Poems From London

Edited By Kelly Scannell

First published in Great Britain in 2019 by:

Young Writers
Remus House
Coltsfoot Drive
Peterborough
PE2 9BF
Telephone: 01733 890066
Website: www.youngwriters.co.uk

FOREWORD

Here at Young Writers, we love to let imaginations run wild and creativity go crazy. Our aim is to encourage young people to get their creative juices flowing and put pen to paper. Each competition is tailored to the relevant age group, hopefully giving each pupil the inspiration and incentive to create their own piece of creative writing, whether it's a poem or a short story. By allowing them to see their own work in print, we know their confidence and love for the written word will grow.

For our latest competition Poetry Wonderland, we invited primary school pupils to create wild and wonderful poems on any topic they liked – the only limits were the limits of their imagination! Using poetry as their magic wand, these young poets have conjured up worlds, creatures and situations that will amaze and astound or scare and startle! Using a variety of poetic forms of their own choosing, they have allowed us to get a glimpse into their vivid imaginations. We hope you enjoy wandering through the wonders of this book as much as we have.

CONTENTS

Independent Entries

Ahamefule Uwandu Ekebi (10)   1

Argyle Primary School, Camden

Abdulrahman Thabit Abdi (7)   2
Sumaiyah Fizah (8)   3
Sahibah Zaman (9)   4
Daisha Souenat (8)   5

Cameron House School, Chelsea

Remy Heriot-Walker (9)   6
Alice Craig (7)   7
Fleur Granier-Deferre (9)   8
Michela Graham (9)   9
Oscar Jackson-Morton (7)   10
Thomas Cagle (9)   11
Scarlett Rose Graham (7)   12
Emma Craig (9)   13
Henry Butterworth (7)   14
Clivia Toepfer (7)   15
Theodore Stankov (9)   16
Yiannis Theofilopoulos (9)   17
Roya Ahsani (7)   18

Heath House Preparatory School, Lewisham

Edwin Mayers (7)   19

Northview Primary School, Neasden

Shania Morgan Aikens (7)   20
Aroush Butt (7)   22

Yanna Halai (10)   23
Usman Ahmad (10)   24
Abdullahi Osman (7)   26
Mursal Bahadurshah (11)   27
Lara Bodza Szeghalmi (9)   28
Tyrah Danso-Dixon (10)   29
Jasmine Elmarini (10)   30
Nelly Mohammed (10)   31
Imaan Arshad (10)   32
Sofia Elmarini (9)   33
Mithran Nathan Kesavan (8)   34
Daniel Palomeras (10)   35
Hanna Elmarini (7)   36
Reece Aaron Smith (9)   37
Mustafa Ali (7)   38
Aasiyah Waseem Boota (10)   39
Amal Warsame (10)   40
Dylan Le Filoux Parsons (8)   41

Our Lady Of Lourdes Catholic Primary School, Finchley

Erin Grace Mulholland (10)   42
Isabell Bekken (9)   44
Maleena Shannon Livera (8)   46
Maya Kufel (8)   48
Cassie Mary O'Connell (9)   49
Max Panwar (9)   50
Alex Cunningham (9)   51
Klara Anna Cahill (8)   52
Nicolas Marco (9)   53
Isaac Mgbadiefe (8)   54
Lily Dempster (9)   55
Benjamin Noah Sinnott (9)   56
Emilia Kurowska (9)   57
Ann Le (9)   58

Murphy O'Melia (9) 59
Olis Shala (9) 60
Rocco Mcsweeney (9) 61
Aaron Lukasz Markowicz (8) 62
Luna Gjoleka (9) 63

St Faith's CE Primary School, Wandsworth

Shon-Shon Ursula De Peyer 64
Michele Bradley (10) 66
Michael Richardson-Paima (10) 68
Anneka Louise Magee (10) 70
Nykanen Bobb-Turner (10) 72

St George's Hanover Square Primary School, Mayfair

Emma Bonetti (9) 73
Joshua Aier (9) 74
Zuzanna Mastalerz (9) 75
Isabel Van Bussel (9) 76
João Pereira (9) 77
Sara Coni (9) 78
Kai Howe (10) 79

St Helen's RC Primary School, Plaistow

Alina Gostek (10) 80
Stephanie Bessabro (9) 82
Cameron San Miguel (10) 83
Vilte Marija Vigraityte (11) 84
Ella Valentina Parra (10) 85
Jayden Harlley (10) 86
Kianne Leesa Charley- 88
McKellop (10)
Emilia James (10) 90
Abena Saah (9) 92
Jeffrey Kwame Opoku (10) 94
Oseobulu Ebosele-Park (10) 95
Favour Awe (10) 96
Yohanna Gezaehew (9) 98
Jasmine Louvia Jno Baptiste (10) 99

Layna Jean Joseph (10) 100
Victor Ohaji (10) 102
Valerie Boakye (10) 103
Folarin Oguntuase (10) 104
Emmanuel Mensah (10) 105
Nassmilah Ali (9) 106
Berenice Koomson (9) 107
Loverage Boakye (10) 108
Aibiokunla Elizabeth Idehen (9) 109
Daniel Abisola Kehinde Wole- 110
Romiluyi (9)
Emmanuel Onuh (10) 111
Farrelll Owusu (10) 112
Ronke Omitunde (10) 113
Lance Arcadio (9) 114
George Alexander 115
Andurnache (9)
Philip (9) 116
Joel Ayikumah Okai (7) 117
Scarlett Dalonos (9) 118
Erin Gail De Leon (9) 119
Ciara Leigh Brodeth 120
Abraham (9)
Ashriya Kaur Logan (7) 121
Marvin Kajura-Bogere (9) 122

St Leonard's CE Primary School, Lambeth

Chloe Hamilton (10) 123
Patrick Hanson (10) 124
Miriam Thomas (10) 126
Daniel Govier (10) 128
Mason Davis-West (10) 129
Emma Cox (11) 130
Timilehin Samuel Ojo (11) 131
Rocco Harrison-Hughes (10) 132
Ben Bourne (10) 133
Sarah Qurayshi (10) 134
Delissa Rhone (10) 135
Ruby Coulson (11) 136
Nikola Motycka (10) 137
Shiva Vishnu Govinden (10) 138
Alysha-Kyda Musah (10) 139

Theodore Bailey (10) 140
Anna Laura Pereira Alberton (10) 141
Dennis Epoh Moudio (10) 142

Trinity Primary Academy, Wood Green

Erin Guan (8) 143
Aleena Khan (9) 144
Lamoy Olarerin (9) 146
Mariam Saada (9) 148
Marsilda Peposhi (10) 149
Luna Tomas (9) 150
Vanousheh Abdi (9) 151
Katrina Poveda (10) 152
Leah Mpofu (9) 153
Faysal Ghebbache (10) 154
Muhammad Ibrahim Kayani (6) 155

Vauxhall Primary School, Vauxhall

Kemi Ogunnubi-Sime (6) 156
Sibella Harvey (6) 157
Lucas Ngo (6) 158
Courtney Bezzina (6) 159
Dana Meho (6) 160
Aaliyah Taylor (6) 161
Blessing Oluwatofunmi Akinola (6) 162
Marie Moore (6) 163
Yasmin Seisay (7) 164
Guney Yilmaz (6) 165
Joanelle Oppong-Boateng (6) 166
Jonah Ennis (6) 167
Eesah Kyriacou (6) 168
Miyah Morris Doyle (6) 169

Wendell Park Primary School, White City

George Blick (10) 170
Noah Foxwell (9) 171
Jaylen Durojaiye (9) 172

Whittingham Primary Academy, Walthamstow

Mohammod Dua Mahmud Unnoto (10) 173
Chloe Alexandra Bray (9) 174
Mary Luggie (10) 176
Anabel Amaka Chinedu (10) 178
Emma Dervishi (9) 180
Luis James Calde (9) 182
Alexander Chan Krinickas (8) 183
David Tinculescu (8) 184
Daniel Brace Carmona (9) 185
Antonio Georoiav (9) 186
Stacey Li (8) 188
Bodhi-Rae Breathnatch (7) 190
Kacper Kajetan Baginski (8) 192
Scarlett Chan (7) 194
Miran Beter (9) 195
Joris Kasperavicius (7) 196
Gabby Bonsu (8) 197
Mariama Abdiwahab (10) 198
Adam Aziz (10) 199
Alev Ekrem (9) 200
Mahira Shara (9) 201
Shayma Mohammed (9) 202
Leovardo Daniel Jayden Thompson (7) 203
Anis Chebbab (9) 204
Taybah Zainab Shah (9) 206
Sirena Hinds (8) 207
Martha Elsie Sennett (8) 208
Kayden Cooke (7) 209
Mia Bondzie (8) 210
Youcef Kaizra (8) 211
Nisa Altun (8) 212
Ariana Alexandra Vacaru (7) 213

Chelsea Li (7)   214
Elle May Newman (8)   215
Jameer Cadotco (7)   216
Elitza Georgieva (8)   217
Tamara Kuneva (7)   218

The Poems

Football

F irst you need skills.
O n three, race down.
O h, use your skills.
T ake notice of people around you.
B e dodging people, in and out.
A nd do not cause a foul.
L ead your team forward.
L earn football and be amazing at it!

Ahamefule Uwandu Ekebi (10)

Diving Into The Deep Blue Sea

I went to jump underwater
My mum said no but I ignored her.
"Hush now!" I ignored her.
I grabbed my diamond diving suit,
And went jumping underwater.

I saw a frogfish shouting, "Boo!"
I saw sharks, humpback whales and clownfish too.
I went deeper into the vast sea
And saw a sperm whale with glasses waving at me.

I dived deeper in the deep, blue sea,
I saw coral and lots of algae.
I saw a net flying near,
Was it my mum? Just sailors catching dinner.

Phew! I turned back to see
My mum staring back at me.

Abdulrahman Thabit Abdi (7)
Argyle Primary School, Camden

The River

The river's a rainbow,
Colourful and bright,
Whenever the river sparkles
The colours will collide.

The river's a monster,
Never stops moving,
Within the blink of an eye
The monster's making a tide.

The river's a mermaid,
Always splishes and splashes,
But whenever you go fast
There may be some crashes.

The river's a source of life,
Provides lots of health,
Whenever you need food or water
The river comes to help.

Sumaiyah Fizah (8)
Argyle Primary School, Camden

Once Upon A Dream

Last night I was dreaming,
Gladly, I didn't hear my mum screaming,
But in my dreams, I saw the sunlight gleaming.

In my dreams, I can hear the doves peacefully
tweeting,
I can continuously hear them whilst I am eating,
In my peaceful dream, there is no game of
cheating.

In my dreams, an Oreo milkshake would be
healthy,
In my dreams, you can relax,
But in my dream, you don't need to pay tax.

Sahibah Zaman (9)
Argyle Primary School, Camden

The Giant Rat

Oh my god! What a giant rat!
Looks like a cat.
It lives in the sewers,
Eating lots of chicken skewers.

Its teeth are goofy
And it smells really cheesy.
When it runs, it does smelly farts,
And leaves dirty scratch marks.

Oh my god! What a giant rat!
It's gone under my mat.
Everyone come,
Let's chase it out.

Daisha Souenat (8)
Argyle Primary School, Camden

School

I raise my head
From my comfy bed
Although inside my mind
I've a little dread
For today, I cannot play the fool
Today is serious, today is school.

And now I sit and take a rest
For I know this morning, I've tried my best
I unpack my mother-made lunch,
And watch my classmates as they munch.

School now over and lessons learnt
Prizes won and credits earnt
On my way home at the end of school
It's no longer serious, bring back the fool!

And now it's late, I must retire
This young fool has run out of fire
With lovely cuddles and goodnight said
I rest my head, back in my comfy bed.

Remy Heriot-Walker (9)
Cameron House School, Chelsea

Country Concert

My story begins every weekend
When chirping birds come waltzing around
Full of excitement and high hopes
For fun-filled weekends, great feasts and laughs.

They come in herds of all kinds of colours
Shapes and sizes, do not matter
But quantities are all the better!

I feed them with love - with peanuts
And nice raisins and apples are never turned down
I chat to them with interest
About their latest news and gossip.

They fill my heart with joy and care
As they sing along with dare
Great is my sadness when I have to go
But I do not despair for I know
That soon there will be another show.

Alice Craig (7)
Cameron House School, Chelsea

My Spirit Hamster

My lovely, little hamster,
How sweet and how kind,
Why, oh why, did you have to go blind?
I loved you more than the Earth's contents,
Why did you have to die?
You are now my spirit hamster,
Oh, sweet and how kind,
Why did you leave me behind?
Now I am lonely and sad,
Nothing can make me glad.
My lovely little hamster,
How small and polite,
You were the greatest hamster
With all my delight.
Please come back down to Earth
Before I leave too,
Hamster and human heaven are so different
And far from each other.
Oh, why did you have to die?

Fleur Granier-Deferre (9)
Cameron House School, Chelsea

8

My Trip To The Moon

My trip to the moon
Was so fine and so cool
In my flying car.
You might think it's bizarre
In the great space,
I thought my idea was ace!
It flew me so high
Through the mighty, starry sky,
Whilst I was screaming, "I can fly!"
The moon was so big and fat,
I couldn't think of anything bigger than that!
It was a bit ugly and had spots around it
So I thought it was so scary,
I couldn't stare at it a bit,
But my trip to the moon
Was so fine and so cool,
Instead, I would love to live there
And not go to school.

Michela Graham (9)
Cameron House School, Chelsea

Fairyland

Being a fairy is fine,
Though I would not pay a dime.
Fairyland is amazing
But you still have to do some chasing.
The goblins are creepy
But they're still sneaky.
Once when I saw them, they were playing the
drums,
They were also blowing bubblegum.
When I asked to be a friend,
They shook their heads and went round the bend.
It made me so sad
But I was so mad.
Lola and Lilly were here
They said to have no fear.
Jack Frost is on the move,
So smooth, smooth, smooth!

Oscar Jackson-Morton (7)
Cameron House School, Chelsea

October 31st

As I stepped outside, I saw that it was dark.
I could hear my heart pumping.
I walked to the first house.
I saw a shadow.
It was a ghost.
It jumped on me.
I ran.
As I walked down the road, I saw a witch
She flew over me.
At the next house, there was a giant spider
Hanging from the balcony.
As I turned around the corner,
I saw a gang of zombies,
They ran after me.
I ran.
It was cold.
It was scary.
It was exciting.
It was Halloween.

Thomas Cagle (9)
Cameron House School, Chelsea

Dancing On Jupiter

On a quiet, sunny day
I said to my sister, "Hey!
Let's go to space and play!"
So we went on our rooftop
And jumped in the blue sky so high!
We found ourselves in
The empty darkness of space
And then all of a sudden,
We heard a *whoosh* and a *swoosh!*
Glittering, shiny stars were shooting past us,
So we tried to get hold of one
And ouch, it burned!
But it's a small price to pay
If you want to be dancing on Jupiter.

Scarlett Rose Graham (7)
Cameron House School, Chelsea

A Woodland Day

Deep in the woodland
Away from prying eyes
Animals have a playdate
With no victims around.

Who are they?
A hedgehog sitting on a log
A fox playing in a bog
A squirrel having a quarrel
Over a juicy nut.

The rabbits are in a habit
Of chatting away
What to feed on in winter, every day.

That is what they get up to
What else could they do?
Planning mischief
For the next day.

Emma Craig (9)
Cameron House School, Chelsea

A UFO Comes To Town

Oh no, oh no, it's a UFO!
What should we do?
Where should we go?
... I don't know!

Aliens are scary
Aliens are strange
Aliens don't like us
Everything will change.

The king came out of his ship
He dove into the Thames
For a quick dip.

He smiled as he went
We have nothing to fear.

Thank goodness
Thank goodness
The friendly aliens are here.

Henry Butterworth (7)
Cameron House School, Chelsea

The Giant Puppy

Me and my cat were walking on the street
When suddenly, there came a witch holding meat.
I quickly grabbed the meat for my cat
The witch got angry so she called the nasty bat.
The nasty, black bat swooped down and bit me
And the witch shouted, "Turn you into a giant puppy!"
The witch disappeared, the cat took the puppy for a walk
Suddenly, the puppy was gone.
When he was back again, he could talk.

Clivia Toepfer (7)
Cameron House School, Chelsea

Orange

I'm an orange
Yes, I'm an orange
As orange as can be
I glisten in the sun
And no one dares eat me because
It would be a shame to eat my beauty
I tell the other oranges but they don't listen
But one day, a man came and gobbled me up!
Now I sit in his belly with the rest of his food.

Theodore Stankov (9)
Cameron House School, Chelsea

The Talking Tree

I was walking in the park
I heard a sound, it sounded funny
I followed the sound, I came to a tree
The tree was talking and playing on his phone
The tree told me, "Go away, a storm is coming."
I went home and there was a huge storm
The tree was right.

Yiannis Theofilopoulos (9)
Cameron House School, Chelsea

Amazing Aliens

A mazing aliens
L ightning fast aliens
I ntelligent aliens
E cstatic, runaway aliens
N utty aliens crashed their spaceship
S uper spaceship goes around the world.

Roya Ahsani (7)
Cameron House School, Chelsea

The Rainbow Star World

The Rainbow Star World is a place full of magic.

A place with pots and wishes
A place with birds, butterflies, unicorns and pretty dishes
Phoenixes and griffins flying in the sky.

Magic is spread all around,
Magic is everywhere, it will always be found.

Rainbow power, I share with you
I hope the magic star shines bright on you too.

Edwin Mayers (7)
Heath House Preparatory School, Lewisham

The Ugly Goblin

In the big, green house
With a great, big nose
Lived an ugly goblin.
He was big and green
And he had yellow teeth
With his great, big mouth,
And his great, big snout.
He looked at you with his great, big frown.
He had no friends and he had no family
And he had no hair.
Can you believe?
No one cared and he was so sad
But very mad.
Do you like goblins?
Because I don't and it is
Because of their attitude
He's very gross.
They eat humans and cows
But they won't eat anything else
They're always messy
And that's why they smell.

They are so rude and they love their food
Because they have nothing to do.
Now I've told you what he can do
You better run because he's after you!
But before you go,
I need to tell you one more thing.
He doesn't like noise
So you should scream and shout
And don't doubt!

Shania Morgan Aikens (7)

Northview Primary School, Neasden

The Talking Cupcake

T he cupcake had a friend who was a talking rainbow,
H e was the only rainbow in the world,
E maa was the cupcake's name.

T he treasure is to be found at the end of the rainbow,
A nd no one knows but only the cupcake,
L ooping colours, leading to treasure,
K nowing that colours can loop us to a beautiful life,
I t would be magical to see this,
N o one had met the scrumptious cupcake
G oing on the adventure to the beauty of life.

C upcakes dancing around the treasure,
U p and down the hill like a kangaroo,
P icking treasure and throwing it in the sky,
C alling out each other's names,
A nd praising each other,
K nowing that friends will always stay friends.
E xcitedly, the cupcakes lived happily ever after.

Aroush Butt (7)

Northview Primary School, Neasden

Surfing On Lava

Red roasting lava gleaming on me,
As I surf through the powerful sea,
The atmosphere is beaming hot,
The thick lava is like soup boiling over from a pot.

I might rapidly sink,
Within a doubtful blink,
I came here for calm peace,
Unfortunately, they treated me as a vicious beast.

Urgh, it's on my surfboard,
Before, I used to feel like a fearless and gruesome
lord,
There is really nothing else to do
Except try to fix my loose shoe.

I cannot wait to escape,
As I perform a really loud shout,
"Why did I begin?" I screamed.
Suddenly, I realised it was all a dream.

Yanna Halai (10)
Northview Primary School, Neasden

The Night Of Terror

I walked in the house
As I saw a mouse
Floorboards creaking
I was freaking
Bats flying
I wasn't crying
Chairs collapsing
My feelings were daunting
My hair was raising
As my blood was curdling
So many books on fire
Just outside the window
Monsters charged like Ludo
Running across the platform
Bats flew around
Like wasps and bees in their hive
I made my run
As the door shut in my face
A wolf smelt my scent
I knew I was dead

As the werewolf glared at me
And growled
I crossed my heart and
Prayed I wouldn't die
The next minute, my life ended...

Usman Ahmad (10)
Northview Primary School, Neasden

Headless Chicken

There is a crazy, clever, headless chicken in a big, fat costume.
There is a crazy robot that always burps and farts.
There is a shark, dancing, shaking his butt.
When the headless chicken thought about making a fart and a burp
Finally, it worked but it was like a human's butt.
The dancing shark danced and he farted.
That was his first-time fart.
The robot's name is Roble and the headless chicken's name is Elmi
And the dancing shark is named Rida.
The shark is a fat one, not a hungry shark
The robot loves to play video games.
He hates to pay for video games.

Abdullahi Osman (7)
Northview Primary School, Neasden

My Scrumptious, Speaking Sweets

Chocolate is very sweet
And very, very good to eat
I really, really like it
Especially for me to try it.

Sweets are very nice
I don't need anyone to ask me twice
To go and take a lovely bite
Or else I'd be there all through the night.

I am going to tell you a secret
That you may not have known
But please let me finish
And do not groan.

Sweets have ears, noses and mouths,
And some even live in the east, north or south
So next time, if you go to the shop
Pick the talking ones
And make sure you don't swap!

Mursal Bahadurshah (11)
Northview Primary School, Neasden

My Baby Rose Whose Name Was Nose

My baby rose, her name was Nose,
She made me laugh when I went to the bath
I told her to stop when she had replied, "Pop!"
From that day on, I was angry
But my mum told me to be happy.
So I stopped and went to mop,
She asked to help, it was greater to be held
She could be very cheeky but also a bit leaky!
We went to the park
But all of a sudden, she saw Mrs Lark.
Nose had stopped being very naughty
But she was very haughty,
As we went home, she was spot on
And did not stop saying "Pop pop!"

Lara Bodza Szeghalmi (9)
Northview Primary School, Neasden

People

People are different,
People are fun,
People are always hopping along,
They try to be good,
They try to be kind,
But sometimes,
They don't get to those times.

People are ambitious,
Some can be modest,
Some are passionate,
A few,
Generous,
But sometimes,
They don't get to those times.

They can be quite sensible,
Or sincere,
Mostly, they can be a bit silly,
Some famous, some not,
But that's how we roll,
Because we're people.

Tyrah Danso-Dixon (10)
Northview Primary School, Neasden

Candy Land

Would you like to enter a land full of treats?
A land made simply of delicious sweets.
Squishy, soft marshmallows, gooey toffee,
Strawberry flavour lollies as tall as a tree.

Piles of mints for you to chew,
Sweet smelling fudge, just for you!
Fluffy light candyfloss as soft as wool,
Eat as much as you like until you are full.

Colourful Smarties as round as a ball,
Red, purple, blue, green, yellow, all.
Chocolate buttons are circles of fun,
Come to my land and you can have one.

Jasmine Elmarini (10)
Northview Primary School, Neasden

The Unexpected Mystery?

It's all a mystery how my teddies started talking and stalking.
It all began when I heard whispering
Until the teddy bears felt like sobbing.
Then they started talking, "Does she even care?
And if she does then why is she leaving us in despair?
It's not fair, she chooses her phone over us bears.
She always promises that she will play but always delays.
I wish she was more caring but she never likes sharing her time.
She's stopped playing with us since the age of nine."

Nelly Mohammed (10)
Northview Primary School, Neasden

Breathing Underwater

I opened my eyes to the beautiful sight,
Where colourful fish were dancing in the bright
sun's light.
They were orange, yellow, purple and some also
blue,
They zoomed past me, it was almost like they flew.
Mouths opening and closing to get their breath,
I almost forgot I had the most powerful power
ever.
Well, keep dreaming and dreaming then you'll get
my point,
Never give up and always have hope.

Imaan Arshad (10)
Northview Primary School, Neasden

Animal Wonderland

Cats with stripes and spots,
Cheetahs with lots of dots.
Birds flying in the blue sky,
Oh, how they fly so high!

Colourful butterflies with sparkly wings,
Bluebirds that sing.
Amazing singing monkeys on a tree,
Crocodiles snapping, what can they see?

Zebras as stripy as my hat,
Riding past the hanging bat.
Lions roaring really loud,
Roaring and walking proud.

Sofia Elmarini (9)
Northview Primary School, Neasden

Dreams

Everybody has a dream,
Some are different,
Some are comparable,
A platform for incredible imagination
Or a period full of trepidation,
All are righteous,
None are erroneous
I love my dreams,
They're extra special for me,
They're absolutely
About what I want to be...
An amazing astronaut,
Why don't you join me,
In my future space adventures?

Mithran Nathan Kesavan (8)
Northview Primary School, Neasden

The Plane Journey

It is a plane journey in the morning,
I am yawning.
The plane is going high in the sky,
When I look through the window,
I want to fly.
I am a beautiful bird,
With enormous, bright wings,
With lots of bling.
Up in the sky is a joyful place,
Look at my happy face.
The sky isn't so bright,
As now it is night.

Daniel Palomeras (10)
Northview Primary School, Neasden

Unicorn Land

Unicorns are riding all day,
They love to play.
Pink, purple hair,
You have to stare.

A long horn as high as the sky,
Unicorns that can fly.
They go high in the air
Like a ride at the fair.

Big eyes, a tail too,
Yellow, green and blue.
Colours like the rainbow,
Unicorns, I love you so.

Hanna Elmarini (7)
Northview Primary School, Neasden

Homework Hell

Who will help me with my homework?
Not my mum, she's too dumb
Not my sister, she's a blister
Not my bro, he's too slow
Not my teacher, she's a weird creature
Not my nan, she's too busy with her tan
Who will help me with my homework?
No one can.

Reece Aaron Smith (9)
Northview Primary School, Neasden

Grasshopper Up To Number Eight

Grasshopper one, grasshopper two
Grasshopper hopping on my shoe
Grasshopper three, grasshopper four
Grasshopper knocking on my door
Grasshopper five, grasshopper six
Picking up sticks
Grasshopper seven, grasshopper eight
In the United States.

Mustafa Ali (7)
Northview Primary School, Neasden

Elf Came To My House For Tea

An elf came to my house
With his big, fat mouse
They ate spaghetti
Like a yeti
When they were about to leave
With a big, fat heave
They spotted a bee
With a strong knee
They spotted their mum
With a big, fat tum.

Aasiyah Waseem Boota (10)
Northview Primary School, Neasden

Perfect Planets

I'm on Mars
I can see the stars
It's so much fun
I can see the sun
Be on Pluto
I'd rather watch Naruto
Actually, Pluto is not a planet
But don't panic
Neither is the sun
But it's still fun.

Amal Warsame (10)
Northview Primary School, Neasden

Plan Of The Pirates

Open the chest
To a diamond quest
Inside you will see
A sparkling ruby
An emerald shining its green light
An opal, colourful and bright
A tiger eye watching
Pirates, beware, fight for your share.

Dylan Le Filoux Parsons (8)
Northview Primary School, Neasden

Halloween Lane

Halloween is right around the corner,
31st of October,
"Boohoo!" everyone shouts
But for us in our land, Halloween is super!

"Trick or treat?" I say,
Tick, tick goes the clock, midnight strikes,
Pitch-black and it's night
But pumpkins show us light.

Vampires and ghosts, skeletons and pumpkins,
"Rumpelstiltskin is lurking in the cemetery," says
the clown,
This town is haunted, haunted by what?
You're about to find out...
"Arghhhh!" I scream.
"Arghhhh!" you scream.

The full moon gleams,
"Do you want to play?" the doll asks.
"No, I don't!" I scream.
The zombies shout.

Is the apocalypse starting again?
Run away, apple dunking, disco dancing.
The mummies are awakening,
The rats scuttle and rattle.

The sewers are blocked and rocked,
Frankenstein says,
"Who wants a hug?"
While the bats eat the bugs.

The mortals are put to sleep,
They should keep their teddies close
As nobody knows
What's about to come, ha ha ha!

Erin Grace Mulholland (10)
Our Lady Of Lourdes Catholic Primary School, Finchley

Dreams

Hurricane! Hurricane!
Hide for shelter,
It's over there,
It's right there,
You can hear the swishing and swashing of the
howling wind,
Arghhhh! Help, I am stuck!
Am I in a small cottage or hut?
No time to ask questions
Oh no,
It's here, it's here,
Where do I go?
Up or down?
I'll probably be hurricane stew by now,
Why am I alive?
This is strange,
I should be dead!
I am in a hurricane,
Am I superhuman?
Oh my God!
Wait!

That's Mum,
She's shouting, "School time!"
But there's no school,
What?
"Wake up, wake up!"
There goes Mum again,
Wait!
Am I asleep?
I must be,
Au revoir future me.

Isabell Bekken (9)
Our Lady Of Lourdes Catholic Primary School, Finchley

The Very Odd Day

It was a very odd day,
The day was all grey,
There was a group of girls,
They were eating cinnamon swirls,
They were watching the telly
When suddenly some wiggly jelly
Appeared and then it said,
"Run to the shed!"
They saw a deep sea,
They fell in and flee.
Suddenly, a volcano came,
It had a big flame,
They decided to dive,
They saw a beaver jive
Then they met a big T-rex,
They said, "Hello."
The dino said, "Yellow."
They all laughed and played,
They all had fun, didn't want to say goodbye,
The dino said, "I live nearby."

They all said, "Yay!"
And that's the end of the very odd day.

Maleena Shannon Livera (8)

Our Lady Of Lourdes Catholic Primary School, Finchley

Birds

I see a mountain
That has a peek up high,
And sweet birds, soaring through the sky
Each has a tail, each has a wing,
But none of them have ever seen the moon so big!
They are all bound
But all they do is fall on the ground
They fly and they jump!
But they always fail with a big bump!
Their dream is to touch the big, shiny moon
And whenever they don't, they gloom.

Until one day,
A blackbird said, "I know how to do it, without a gloom!"
"Just say it in your dreams and it will come true."
"Tell us more, tell us more,"
Said the very loud roar.
"That is all I know!"
Said the bird covered in snow
Before he flew away.

Maya Kufel (8)
Our Lady Of Lourdes Catholic Primary School, Finchley

The Thing

Uncle B had always said
A thing lived beneath my bed
That if I didn't curl up small
I'd wake up pinned against the wall.

"Nobody will hear your screams,
From where you're stuck inside your dreams
There is no escape
Unless you learn to deviate."

Feeling scared and oh so small
I tiptoed out across the hall
Goosebumps ran beneath my hair
Like warning bells saying: 'stop right there'.

Looking left and right
To see what was in sight
Oh, how do I get through
The rest of the night?

Cassie Mary O'Connell (9)
Our Lady Of Lourdes Catholic Primary School, Finchley

Cricket Land

Cricket is a fun sport
It is played with bat and ball
There are two teams
Some are very tall.

One bats and the other bowls
The clothes are either white or multicoloured
Is it a sport? It is more than a sport!
Some people say it is a religion!

Have you heard of The Ashes?
Check it out
Cricket is the best
You will never shout.

You play on a big pitch
And you run quite a bit
It is sometimes a long game
But it keeps you fit!

Max Panwar (9)
Our Lady Of Lourdes Catholic Primary School, Finchley

Thunder And Lightning

This is a poem about thunder and lightning,
It is too frightening, the thunder is very heavy
And the lightning is very steady.
Thunder can be a number on a scale out of 100,
In my world, there only is thunder and lightning.
Crack! It's coming! So I started humming
Then I looked at my clock
But all I heard was *tick-tock!*
"Time for bed," Mum said
But the thing I didn't know
Was that it was all inside my head.

Alex Cunningham (9)

Our Lady Of Lourdes Catholic Primary School, Finchley

My Busy Life

Hi, this is my poem
My name is Klara
And my cousin's name is Tara
My brother's name is Daniel and
He looks like a Cocker Spaniel.
I live in Finchley
And if I fall asleep, then pinch me
Milo is my brother
And I love him like no other
My favourite subject is art
And now I need to fart
Our Lady of Lourdes is my school
And it is located near the swimming pool
Earlier, I said hi
Now I should say goodbye.

Klara Anna Cahill (8)
Our Lady Of Lourdes Catholic Primary School, Finchley

The Flying Menace

It was a hot and nice summer day in July
I opened the window to let the air go by
And *swoosh* came a humongous fly
Mum and Dad ran, terrified
My guinea pig stopped squeaking and began
to cry.

I crawled to the kitchen and grabbed a newspaper
Then silently, stalked the fly like a hunter
But it saw me with its thousand eyes and got
scared
The monster hit the windows until it flew away
Leaving my family petrified.

Nicolas Marco (9)
Our Lady Of Lourdes Catholic Primary School, Finchley

The Dragon And The Falling Bridge

The rotten bridge creaks under the train's rapid movement.
Wide-eyed people stare, frightened into the clouds.
Flames flicker then wide nostrils appear.
A sensation of heat and falling comes into focus.
Molten metal, flesh and blood, burning wood falls into the wild ocean.
Grateful sharks feast on the rest of the people.
The dragon flies off into the sky,
Smirking with glee, back to his own land.

Isaac Mgbadiefe (8)

Our Lady Of Lourdes Catholic Primary School, Finchley

Moaning Molly

She sits there all fancy,
Wrapping the teachers round her pinky,
With her put-on cuteness
But really, it's just bogus.

She's just a moaning moose,
Who had been let loose,
From the zoo of annoying,
To torture us with her complaining.

I wish she would stop moaning,
And quit being showy,
If she could stop being a phoney,
She could be nice, our Molly.

Lily Dempster (9)
Our Lady Of Lourdes Catholic Primary School, Finchley

The Dog In The Park

The dog in the park
Chased the squirrel up a tree.

The dog in the park
Chased the ball.

The tall man called
But the dog still chased the ball.

The woman called, "Come on!"
And the dog came back.

The dog chased the dogs
But didn't care about leaving.

The dog in the park
Went to sleep.

Benjamin Noah Sinnott (9)
Our Lady Of Lourdes Catholic Primary School, Finchley

Underwater

Here I am
Under the sparkling sea
Here I am
With a magical creature
Here I am
Looking at her
Here I am
Touching her hair
Here I am
Swimming with her
Here I am
Back in her house
Here I am
Talking to her
Here I am
With a human
Here I am
With a fish
Here I am
With a mermaid.

Emilia Kurowska (9)
Our Lady Of Lourdes Catholic Primary School, Finchley

Fast Food Land

When I walked into the hole
I saw ketchup in a bowl
I thought I had a dream
But there's a real burger stream
The burger's as big as a building
And I want to eat everything
Fries as big as a house
But I am just a little mouse
And then I began to sing
This place is delicious and amazing!

Ann Le (9)
Our Lady Of Lourdes Catholic Primary School, Finchley

Baby Dragon Surprise

One day, I opened my door
To my amazement, there I saw
A jiggling box
I hope it's not a fox
I peeked inside, to my surprise
A dragon, undersized
He had two heads
And he destroyed things to shreds
My baby dragon, half fire, half water
Please don't have a daughter!

Murphy O'Melia (9)
Our Lady Of Lourdes Catholic Primary School, Finchley

Oli's Rap!

My name is Olis and I like olives
Although my eyes are green, they go with my jeans
My fish is called Tiger and he likes figures
My friend is Max and he likes Tic Tacs.
I just wanted to add that my teacher is fab,
And she is very good in doing the Dab
I hope that you enjoyed my rap!

Olis Shala (9)
Our Lady Of Lourdes Catholic Primary School, Finchley

Fortnite

There once was a boy,
He didn't like toys.

But he loved to play Fortnite,
He got into the top fights.

He wasn't very bright,
Played late into the night.

Obsessed with this game,
Online with his name,
Survival was his fame.

Rocco Mcsweeney (9)
Our Lady Of Lourdes Catholic Primary School, Finchley

Holidays!

Days of fun and play
Always a bit too short
Fun and laziness of any sort!

Swimming, playing, everything cool
No homework and no school!
Nights away and longer days
Back to school, goodbye holidays!

Aaron Lukasz Markowicz (8)
Our Lady Of Lourdes Catholic Primary School, Finchley

A Magical Pound

I look up, I look down, I look around.
I see a magic ground,
Where there is a pound.
A pound that goes around,
A pound that's round and round.
It shimmers on the ground.
The pound made a sound.

Luna Gjoleka (9)
Our Lady Of Lourdes Catholic Primary School, Finchley

The Scorpther

(Based on 'The Jabberwocky' by Lewis Carroll)

'Twas bitterish and the gloomy pines,
Did shacrumble and dripptle in the stale,
All mothy were the tangtwives,
And the Ditherys Olpale.

"Beware the Scorpther, my dear son!
The teeth that snap, the sting that's pain,
Beware the Jub-Jub Bird and shun,
The derocious Bandersmain."

He took his fatal scythe in hand,
Long time the poisecalthy foe he seek,
So pondered he by the tall Tum-Tum tree,
Still as a mountain peak.

And as in tentative thought he stood.
The stealthy Scorpther, sting of blame,
Came streaking through the fiery wood,
And gronicked as it came!

One two! One two! And pew, pew through,
The deadly edge want zing, zang, spack!

He left it quartered with the heart of the
slaughtered,
He went galomping back!

"And has thou slain the savage Scorpther?
Come to my arms, my triumphant boy,
Oh wonderful day! Hooray hallay!"
He griffawed in his glee.

'Twas bitterish and the gloomy pines,
Did shacrumble and dripptle in the stale,
All mothy were the tangtwives,
And the Ditherys Olpale.

Shon-Shon Ursula De Peyer
St Faith's CE Primary School, Wandsworth

The Pekka-Jockey

(Based on 'The Jabberwocky' by Lewis Carroll)

'Twas Drappy and the hawering Draps
Didn't craft and mine
In the laps
All the Retals of mine,
Are the endangers of Labthend,
And the Pekkas mercilessly slayed.

"Beware the Pekka-Jockey, my son!
The swords that stab, his eyes that spell!
And they killed as hot as the sun.
You will be victorious or taken to hell!"

He took his diamond sword in hand,
Long time, the ultra foe he fought
So he murdered the Tum-Tum tree,
Died in mid-thought.

And as in blackened thought he died
A knight with an emerald sword
Came murdering through Tugley-Wood with a slide,
He slaughtered the Pekka-Jockey and became bored.

"Hast thou slain the Pekka-Jockey?
Come to my arms, my beamish knight!
Who gave you that sword like hell?"
He laughed in his light.

'Twas Drappy and the hawering Draps
Did craft and mine
In the laps
All the Retals of mine,
Were the endangers of Labthend
And the knights mercilessly slayed.

Michele Bradley (10)
St Faith's CE Primary School, Wandsworth

The Drocfy

(Based on 'The Jabberwocky' by Lewis Carroll)

'Twas cold and the flouter cave,
Did nurture and killed in the phase,
All mumbly and manky was the Voltave,
And the villagers did moan in a cage.

"Beware the Drocfy my son,
The jaws that kill, the paws with speed
Beware the Pandor and shun
The mysterious thing on pills."

And as in ignorance, he stood
The Drocfy with eyes of flame,
Came stomping through the battered wood,
And imitated as it came.

One, two! One, two! He sliced and diced,
The lethal weapon with one sharp swing,
He left it dead and took it home,
He went gulumphing back.

"What has happened to my ignorant boy?
Come outside and take a look

It can't be the Drocfy with eyes of flame
You have killed it, I am amazed!"

'Twas cold and the flouter cave,
Did nurture and killed in the phase,
All mumbly and manky was the Voltave,
And the villagers did moan in a cage.

Michael Richardson-Paima (10)
St Faith's CE Primary School, Wandsworth

The Slithergony

(Based on 'The Jabberwocky' by Lewis Carroll)

'Twas sketchy and the grimy cave
Did groan and moan in the pape
All brilling were the toemoe
And the timemare and maves.

"Beware the Slithergony, my boy
He eats most and sees all
Beware the Dub-Dub Bird and chun
The Frumious Bandersnatch!"

He took his viple sword in hand
"Stand back!" he said and stood
And thought as he rested by the Tum-Hum tree
And stood a while in horror.

And as in uffish thought he stood
The Slithergony with eyes of evilness
Came whiffling through the Tungel Wood
And stomped as it came.

One two! One two!
And through and through

The viple sword went snicker, snacker
He left it dead and with its leg
He went hanging back.

'Twas sketchy and the grimy cave
Did groan and moan in the pape
All brilling were the toemoe
And the timemare and maves.

Anneka Louise Magee (10)
St Faith's CE Primary School, Wandsworth

The Eyes Of Destruction

The eye of the storm, Zeus stares, Poseidon glares,
Lightning bolts attack the ocean as waterspouts
strike the sky.

The eye of the gods,
Its golden glare, its eagle-like stare, the eye that
cares.

The eye of emotion,
Tears of neglect, roars of anger, groans of
depression
A swirl of emotion.

The eye of winter,
Its frozen glare, its snow-like stare,
Vanquishing the essence of warmth.

The eye of power,
Its dangerous stare, its threatening glare
Tendrils of destruction.

So...
"Don't blink, don't stare, don't glare but
Don't look into the eyes of destruction."

Nykanen Bobb-Turner (10)
St Faith's CE Primary School, Wandsworth

Halloween Land

Welcome to Halloween Land
Where a zombie doesn't have a hand,
Where the magic comes to life
And a monster has a knife!
And a sweet
Is not a treat,
Where spooky things,
Like a bat, has wings!
Where there is a spooky ghost,
Or at least most,
There is a wood,
That is as dark as when you are under a black
hood!
There is a vampire,
That lives in the fire,
There is a spider,
That is a perfect finder,
There is a pumpkin that is blue
That has the shape of a shoe,
So Halloween Land is
Freaky and creepy.

Emma Bonetti (9)
St George's Hanover Square Primary School, Mayfair

Aeroplane Sheriff

Oi aeroplane, what are you doing?
Just practising playing my trumpet.
Oi aeroplane, what are you doing?
Just playing with my pet.
Oi aeroplane, what are you doing?
Just eating my crumpet.
Oi aeroplane, what are you doing?
You just woke me up from bed!
Oi aeroplane, what are you doing?
I almost banged my head!
Oi aeroplane, what are you doing?
This is my shed!
Oi aeroplane, what are you doing?
My pig is dead!

Joshua Aier (9)
St George's Hanover Square Primary School, Mayfair

Dumbo

Wow! I woke up in a jungle,
There were so many animals,
I found an elephant
His name was Dumbo,
He asked me to paint his nails,
I said, "With what?"
"With nail polish please."
"What colour?"
"Rainbow please."
"Okay."
"Wait, pink please."
"Okay!"
He squiggled and wiggled
But somehow it worked, wow!

Zuzanna Mastalerz (9)

St George's Hanover Square Primary School, Mayfair

The Animal Disco

There was once an animal disco
With a young bear playing a cello,
A young racoon playing the drums,
The audience dropped lots of crumbs,
The animals stayed up all night,
Well actually, you'd think they might.
In the end, they all were happy
'Til the baby mouse peed in her nappy.

Isabel Van Bussel (9)
St George's Hanover Square Primary School, Mayfair

Pool Of Lava

I went to a pool of lava
With my friend, Larva!
I stayed there some time
But Mr Larva said, "Fine!"

Just when Mr Larva said, "Please!"
The whole pool did freeze
We stayed there a little bit
But that's the end of it.

João Pereira (9)
St George's Hanover Square Primary School, Mayfair

Neverland Witches

We are a witch group
From Neverland
We like to make poison
From a red dragon's hand
We admire our master
As she lets us travel
Ha, ha, ha!
We are the witches from Neverland.

Sara Coni (9)
St George's Hanover Square Primary School, Mayfair

The Fox

A Kennings poem

A meat-eater
A night-lurker
A good-smeller
A pee-speeder
A night-traveller
A night-hunter
A bin-digger
A food-stealer.

Kai Howe (10)

St George's Hanover Square Primary School, Mayfair

Farting Queen

In a palace far, far away
You wouldn't want to go there anyway
If you want to ask me why
Well, the stinky smell makes you cry.

You might want to know what it is
It's the crazy Queen Fart Fizz
The story started in a crazy way
When the farting queen wanted to play.

She didn't know what to do
In their heads, the big baked bean idea grew
The challenge was easy
Eat as much as you can.

The farting queen wanted to win
So she ate a thousand tins of beans
Now she farts out a smelly bubble
Toot!

Now she's famous all over the world
Even ABBA's singers from Sweden sing about her

"You are the farting queen
Young and sweet
Only seventeen
Farting queen..."
"You can fart, you can jive
Having the time of your life..."

Alina Gostek (10)
St Helen's RC Primary School, Plaistow

The Best Candy World

On Candy World, Candy World,
As I walked up the hill, I raised my head
And saw something as beautiful
And colourful as a rainbow.
I got closer and it was rainbow candy.
I ate all of the colours of the rainbow,
Red, orange, yellow, green, blue, indigo and violet.

I was so happy eating the rainbow candy I had
Dimple, oh sweet rainbow candy,
Oh, what a sweet candy world.
When I got to Candy World
I played Candy Crush on my chocolate phone,
What a lovely game it was.

There were talking cupcakes that wore gold
And silver beads that can be eaten.
I saw a gingerbread man
Running down the hill.

At the end of the rainbow
There was a river of milkshake
And a Milky Way that led to a pot of gold.

Stephanie Bessabro (9)

St Helen's RC Primary School, Plaistow

Henry's Habit

Henry, my weird friend, has a habit!
He's been practising for years and months,
He buys French fries and stuffs them in his ears
and his nose.

I ask him why, he just shakes his head and may not
even know,
It's just a thing my friend started a long time ago.

It's slightly gross and silly and obviously strange
And for his birthday, he's going to a firing range,
It's difficult to change, he's lately come up with a
new idea, to put two up his nose.

It's even grosser, I suppose,
Why would you put French fries up your nose
And stand there in a cringy pose?

A few days later, he came to my house
And told me why he puts them in his ears and
nose.
He said, "For brain food."

Cameron San Miguel (10)
St Helen's RC Primary School, Plaistow

The Pineapple Who Ate My Dragon

"Oh Pineapple, Pineapple," Mrs Potato said,
"How could it not be possible to tidy your bed?"
"I don't know," he said.
Then ran away with a hungry belly and met the
dragon, Telly.
He looked away and could not believe it, that Telly
was in his belly.
Mrs Potato ran for her life but all she could think of
was her son ate a dragon!
She took the needle and, "Arghhhh!" she
screamed.
All she had seen was nothing but a bean,
She said, "My son is a bean!
Not any seed, a pineapple bean!
He is back to baby size
I should have fixed my eyes.
But hopefully the dumb dragon, Telly
Will never be in his belly again
Now I hope the seed does not break and bend
And that's the end."

Vilte Marija Vigraityte (11)
St Helen's RC Primary School, Plaistow

I Ate Voldemort

He wriggled and wiggled inside me
His sorcerer's spells sizzled in my belly
He tasted quite nice!
But he is the opposite in real life
Love Harry Potter
I did his job
I thought his real name was Bob!
But turns out they fired him
And left it at that
Inside me, Voldemort was a vicious killing machine
He eventually came out but at the wrong end
That was the end of us being friends
Whilst he was inside, I sneezed an evil spell
Sparkling spells forced their way through somehow
It went a little like this, "Avada Kedavra!"
Can you keep a secret?
I killed someone with that spell
They fainted and fell
With that, I flee
It was nearly half past three
And it was time for my tea!

Ella Valentina Parra (10)
St Helen's RC Primary School, Plaistow

People As Emus

Imagine being an emu
Because you don't look any new
You see someone handsome
But they hold you for ransom
Wake up people, you guys are emus!
Imagine being an emu
Because you don't look any new
You look down at the desert
And you see feathers
Then you look up in the misty sky
But all you see is a great, big pie!
You then look down below
But your shadow is slow.
Soon, you turn your neck around
Like you're going homeward bound
Feathers covering up all of you
Until you know who!
You scream and shout but nothing comes out
Why am I in a nightmare?

My life continues as an emu
Anyway, I'll just go to the loo
Where it's not in a zoo!

Jayden Harlley (10)
St Helen's RC Primary School, Plaistow

Clock Head Rhyme

Clock time, this story will rhyme
Clock Head jumps
Wham! Bam! Pump!
"Ow!" says Scientist Unicorn
His horn, it cracked...
He had it since he was born
Now what's going to happen
Can't you see a pattern?
Poor, poor man
It's like he got hit by a pan!
The darkness in his eyes was overtaking
And the only thing Clock Head was thinking
About was time racing.

The trees went by
The skies were saying bye
And the story has yet to come!

A wishing fairy appears
Clock Head takes a year
Just to wish for a thumb
Look, look, there is Scientist Unicorn

He got up all old and wrinkly
And his feet got all tinkly.

Kianne Leesa Charlery-McKellop (10)

St Helen's RC Primary School, Plaistow

The Heaven Concert

La, la, la,
Goes the angel
Flapping his wings up and down.
Every single day he does it,
All around the town.
There's also a pig
Always singing, 'Gold Porkchop'
But he doesn't even live up in Heaven!
But I understand, he's only seven,
"Why can't he come and live with us?"
Complained the chicken nugget angel.
I'll just wait and wait and wait,
And I'll be eating a bagel.
"Ahem, ahem,
Allow me to introduce myself,
I'm the chicken nugget angel,
Pleasure to finally meet you!"
La, la, la,
Goes the angel
Flapping his wings up and down.

All the time they do it,
Him and Mr Pig!

Emilia James (10)
St Helen's RC Primary School, Plaistow

Bubble

One day, Lilly Rose
Flew in a bubble
It was a big hubble,
Flying and flying,
Through the air,
Bump and bump into trees,
Flying up and down all the way,
Side to side, jumping high,
It flew and flew and flew
Into the sky, up and up and up,
Yum, yum, that was a nice cloud,
"Look at the rainbow in the sky!"
Pop, pop, pop!
The bubble went down
And down and down,
She went until she fell into Cookie World.
Lilly Rose saw cookies everywhere,
Cookies and cookies and cookies.
She ate and ate and ate,
She saw a house
Made out of pink hot chocolate.

Suddenly, she woke up,
It was a dream, dream, dream.

Abena Saah (9)
St Helen's RC Primary School, Plaistow

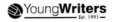

Back To The Past Dinosaur Dimension

The fierceness with razor claws,
An eating machine with big, fat jaws,
Badly behaved, you cannot resist,
I had to use my small, little fist.

A wondrous roar,
Made the waterfalls pour,
Remember those jaw-clashing teeth,
He won't let you breathe.

With my big discovery,
I came back with a recovery,
It reaches and rages with royal roars
With those monstrous teeth, no one ignores.

Everything I saw, I had to make an enquiry,
If it was true, I would write it in my diary,
I was filled with determination,
So people could follow my inspiration,
He is the king of all the dinosaurs,
The tyrannosaurus tex. *Roar!*

Jeffrey Kwame Opoku (10)
St Helen's RC Primary School, Plaistow

This Game Sucks

I was just playing games, sitting on my chair,
Not having the tiniest care,
But then, my TV sparked
And I was getting sucked in,
If I survive this, I'm throwing my really expensive TV
in the bin.

I couldn't hold on much longer,
I got sucked into what seemed to be my game,
I'm playing Fortnite, and I'm not dying in shame!
Long story short, I got a Victory Royale,
The intensity of the match really raised my morale.

Another portal, (oh yeah, a portal came
out of my TV which sucked me in),
Came out and again, I got sucked in,
I got back into reality and like I promised,
I threw my TV in the bin.

Oseobulu Ebosele-Park (10)
St Helen's RC Primary School, Plaistow

Resurrection On Earth

Wake up! Wake up!
The day has come.
Stand up! Stand up!
No time to hum.

The chain has been broken,
Our ancestors have awoken.
We're going to have a party
To show the devil he should be sorry.

Great Grandma!
Great Grandpa!
You're alive!
Have fun during the party tonight.

We danced and danced the night away
And I think we sure wanted everyone to stay.
There was food and all kinds of stuff,
We ate and ate 'til we stuffed ourselves up.

The party was finally over
But it's not good to be a groaner

Because who knows what we'll discover
From a little pinch of the nose...

Favour Awe (10)
St Helen's RC Primary School, Plaistow

Dad In Wonderland!

In a place called Wonderland,
There is something fun to be planned,
But there is something weird lurking around,
My dad, of course!

My dad, who is a wizard, is very weird,
Who has a long, grey beard,
He is never really crazy
But sometimes very lazy.

He has a pet dragon
Who is always being mischievous,
His name is Freaky Free
But make sure you keep your food away.

My dad always likes to use his magic,
It really never ends up tragically,
It is like he can hear
The magic whisper in his ear.

I am warning you to stay away,
I bet you would rather play.

Yohanna Gezaehew (9)
St Helen's RC Primary School, Plaistow

Bubbles Turning Into Candy!

It begins in a world full of bubbles...
Which could turn into anything, especially candy.
There was a girl called Jasmine and she saw the bubbles
She wished for the bubbles to turn into candy
She brought some bubble mixture and every time
She wanted candy, she blew a bubble.
Yum! Yum! Yum!
Sweets are so good, who doesn't like sweets?

Chomp! Chomp! Chomp!
"I can't stop eating the bubbles."
They are so yummy
"Please don't eat me Jasmine," said the bubbles.
They are as sweet as juice
These bubbles look like a pink lollipop.

Jasmine Louvia Jno Baptiste (10)
St Helen's RC Primary School, Plaistow

The Girl Who Leapt Through Time!

A girl...
Who can leap through time
Backwards and forwards
To fix things that were wrong,
But she didn't go on a plane
She went the clumsy way on a lane,
Numbers on her arm, fifty and down.
Who knows what happened to her,
We'll never know what.

She fell with a big bang!
When she went somewhere else
She thought it was a joke
So she was giggling like a group of geese.
When she fell, she thought she was as
Clumsy as a blind cat
She also thought she was a clown.

Who knows what happened to her?
If you know,
Tell us now!

Layna Jean Joseph (10)
St Helen's RC Primary School, Plaistow

Whilst Driving A Train To Heaven

Whilst driving a train to Heaven,
I felt like I was a saint!
Flying up into the blue,
To meet God and his friends.
The weather was as placid as a sleeping tiger,
And the clouds majestically bowed at my feet.
The train was as fast as the speed of light,
Whoosh!
Speeding past storks in the sky,
As we wanted to get there quickly.
We wanted our souls to rest
In sheer peace, joy and happiness.
I felt distressed but somewhat responsible,
Because if we crashed, I would be to blame.
So that's why I felt distressed,
Whilst driving a train to Heaven.

Victor Ohaji (10)
St Helen's RC Primary School, Plaistow

Pizzatastic

Pizza, pizza, tasting hot
Pepperoni jumping off
Cheesy, cheesy
Please, please
Pizza, pizza
Smelling delicious
And cheesy
Gooey, ooey cheese, so yummy
Crunchy crust goes in my tummy
Children chop the chewy cheese
Chewy cheese as hot as peas
I like pizza, so do you
Have a piece or maybe two
Make me a pizza if you can
Baked in the oven in a pan
Top it with lots of extra cheese
How many slices will I need?
So come and have a piece of pizza
Pizza, pizza, it's a treat
Pizza, pizza, fun to eat.

Valerie Boakye (10)
St Helen's RC Primary School, Plaistow

Bathing My Pet Dracolyte

Oh my, bathing this Dracolyte
It's like a never-ending World War III
Water and lava, *tut-tut!*
It's not a good mix
Biting, fire-breathing and scratching
Help, I've not even run the water yet
World War III has started
I repeat, it has started!

In a ten-foot bath, my Dracolyte is growling
And he pongs 'til the cows come home
Even though he has a very bad temper
I am going to do what he hates
Which is taking him to the dentist
"Help, I'm gonna be a Sunday roast!"

Folarin Oguntuase (10)
St Helen's RC Primary School, Plaistow

The Unusual Football Match!

F erocious players panicking

O pen pitch to play on

O f course, it sounds plain as milk

T oday, you'll be amazed

B ut all you have to remember is

A nxious players are crazy like monkeys

L udicrous match to play on

L osers will always be losers.

M ermaids will also play

A llowed on the pitch are hockey sticks

T he rules are no feet or hockey sticks to touch the ball

C heer along with others

H ear the noise and enjoy.

Emmanuel Mensah (10)

St Helen's RC Primary School, Plaistow

My Busy Family

I love my parents a lot,
They give me lots of care,
When I make them proud
They shine as bright as a flare!

My parents are always busy,
They are as strong as the Hulk,
But when they are not busy
They tidy up the bulk!

I love my little brother,
He makes my life complete,
But when I get a sister,
I'll have a little fleet!

My mum is loving and always rushing,
My dad is caring and hard-working,
My brother is helpful and cute,
But that's not the best thing!

Nassmilah Ali (9)
St Helen's RC Primary School, Plaistow

Crazy Poem

Imagine a giant burger as Saturn,
Cookies for asteroids, candy for rockets,
Cheese for the moon,
They are edible, yum, yum, yum!
It's mind-blowing, it's knowledgeable.

Look at that giant,
He's got a case,
Let's play a game, it's not a race,
If it was I'd be apace.

Have you ever been to an ice rink?
If not, freeze the sink
Or even colour it pink,
Look at that, it's some ink,
I'm just joking, go to Saturn,
You can ride on its icy ring.

Berenice Koomson (9)
St Helen's RC Primary School, Plaistow

Shrinking, Sizzling Soda

Shrinking, sizzling soda
It shrinks and sizzles in your mouth
Just take a sip
But be quick
Before you turn into a stick
Then from a stick into a twig.

It sizzles and shrinks
Makes you feel weird and giddy
And it's amazing.

Shrinking, sizzling soda
It shrinks and sizzles in your mouth
It's fizzy
Makes you feel dizzy
Sizzle! Bam! Pop!
It never stops.

It's just like candy
You can never stop drinking
Just so addictive.

Loverage Boakye (10)
St Helen's RC Primary School, Plaistow

A Trip To The Moon

I used a broom
To go to the moon
My mission was to get a glass of blood
Suddenly, I heard a *thud!*

When I arrived
I was full of pride
Then my belly began to rumble
To find an apple crumble.

I went to the station to deliver the blood
But when I stepped on mud, arghhhh!
My boss' name is Cheeme
That's why we became a team.

I went on my broom
To go to my crew
I felt like doing a poo
Then I saw a toilet and went right through.

Aibiokunla Elizabeth Idehen (9)
St Helen's RC Primary School, Plaistow

The Singing Volcano

There was a singing volcano
It sang the right notes but knocked over a boat
It let out lava when it shouted
At people who made fun of its voice.

It loved singing but when it was extremely angry
It would make an earthquake
And make lava come out rapidly.

Well as if by magic, it started to suck lava back up
Then he started singing again
Then a wizard appeared and said,
"You won't have lava but you will have water."

Daniel Abisola Kehinde Wole-Romiluyi (9)
St Helen's RC Primary School, Plaistow

Football As A Car

Football is a good sport,
You kick a ball
Then score a goal
And celebrate, "Hooray hooray!"

The football is as glossy as a car,
And looks pleasant.
You might play football,
Wait in the car.

Football is a good sport,
Helping others,
When they're injured
And kicking the ball off the car.

Tackling very hard
Then helping them up
And cheating to win,
Always scoring in the car, yeah!

Emmanuel Onuh (10)
St Helen's RC Primary School, Plaistow

Cats Take Over The World

We said hi hi to the cats
And bye bye to the rats,
In a world surrounded by miaow
Certainly not by cows.

Cats are flying
Rats are crying
We all fall down.

Down to the pit of cookies
Surrounded by rookies
We all just want to *munch, munch, munch!*
While I just sit and *crunch, crunch, crunch!*

Looking across, seeing the trees curled
Wondering how on Earth did the cats
Take over the world.

Farrelll Owusu (10)
St Helen's RC Primary School, Plaistow

Blazing Hot

I climb off my motorbike
And start to hike.
To that amazing spot,
Bright and dazzling,
Gorgeous and hot.

I cast out my towel
And start to howl.
Sunglasses, umbrella
I'm ready for this weather.

Big, round, yellow ball
Blazing rays around the pool.
It's getting hot, I'm about to rot.
Dripping, dropping, like a topping
It's getting hot, I'm about to pop!

Ronke Omitunde (10)
St Helen's RC Primary School, Plaistow

Travel Through Time And Space

This certain meteor burns all planets
Bouncing off them when I'm on it
It would roll off Saturn's ring
When we're all in mourning.

The next is Uranus,
Which is considered funny
It's on its way to Earth
But it's still hitting Pluto.

Oh no, it's coming to Earth
Boom! Earth shakes, it stops,
Yes, it's in the ocean,
Too bad it destroyed the moon.

Lance Arcadio (9)
St Helen's RC Primary School, Plaistow

Console Land

You've got everything you need,
Xbox, PlayStation, TV,
Have a takeaway for free,
Take away the games you play.

Once you're in, you're in for real,
And the life becomes unreal.

Fortnite and Minecraft is a good combination
Where boys and girls begin the competition.

You explore new lands and battle opponents,
Fortnite trees dance all day and save the game
today.

George Alexander Andurnache (9)
St Helen's RC Primary School, Plaistow

Skydiving Into Hot Chocolate

What is that Dad?
What's that?
The pool,
Oh, it's a hot chocolate pool,
It's very cool,
I can skydive in there
This is a fair,
Yay!
Hooray!
I am going to drink the hot chocolate
Yay!
OMG, this is nice,
This is what I like,
It's hot and you can drink,
Come right in,
Yay, hooray!
Let's go to the hot chocolate parade.

Philip (9)
St Helen's RC Primary School, Plaistow

SpongeBob's Facts

Who is the one that lives in a pineapple house?
SpongeBob SquarePants!
Who is the one that lives under the sea?
SpongeBob SquarePants!
And that has a starfish friend?
SpongeBob SquarePants!
Is funny, kind and friendly, also clumsy as well?
SpongeBob SquarePants!
Is friendly with Squidward, Patrick the Starfish
Mr Krabs and Sandy Squirrel?
SpongeBob SquarePants!

Joel Ayikumah Okai (7)
St Helen's RC Primary School, Plaistow

Rainbows, Rainbows

Rainbows, rainbows
The colourful colours
Look like flowers
The wonderful sky up high
I wish it could rain Skittles
When the rainbow is up high
I hope I could fly
By the rainbow.

Rainbows, rainbows
What are rainbows?
They are colourful colours
Up high by the clouds
When it's rainy and sunny
It pops out of nowhere
In the world!

Scarlett Dalonos (9)
St Helen's RC Primary School, Plaistow

My Talking Minifigures

My talking Minifigures
Are so cute,
They're very funny,
Always hungry,
When they are sleeping
Every night
They always dream
Of dancing marshmallows.
Every morning
They hear singing bubbles
Popping so loudly,
They start saying, "Howdy!"
My talking Minifigures
Are so cute,
They are funny,
Always hungry!

Erin Gail De Leon (9)
St Helen's RC Primary School, Plaistow

Riding On Unicorns Wherever You Go

Unicorns are magical
Just like fairies that are mystical
These animals can give you a ride
Wherever you go and fly.

You don't need to moan
Unicorns never groan
They will always be your friend
Forever until the end.

If you are too lazy to walk
Why not talk?
Let's play with magic
To make your day complete.

Ciara Leigh Brodeth Abraham (9)
St Helen's RC Primary School, Plaistow

My Crazy Poem

Walking in the ocean with my giraffe,
It felt so good, I was full of emotion.
The waves were hitting the giraffe
Like he was having a bath
And then he started to laugh.
Now my crazy adventure has come to an end,
Goodbye Mr Giraffe, my very tall friend.

Ashriya Kaur Logan (7)
St Helen's RC Primary School, Plaistow

Fortnite Poem

Fortnite, Fortnite, Fortnite
It's so much fun
I land at Tilted
Grab a gun
Oh no!
A guy
I'm done
Play more and more
Until I'm really done
And at the end,
I say, "That was fun
Let's play some more!"

Marvin Kajura-Bogere (9)
St Helen's RC Primary School, Plaistow

St Leonard's Is My Home

St Leonard's,
My school, my family, my home
If I weren't here, I would rather be alone.
St Leonard's,
My school, my family, my home
This school will stand like stone.
St Leonard's,
My school, my family, my home
They will know what to do when I'm feeling sad.
St Leonard's,
My school, my family, my home
This is the place where I will always feel glad.
St Leonard's,
My school, my family, my home
This is the place with everlasting love
St Leonard's,
My school, my family, my home
This place is as beautiful as a dove.

Chloe Hamilton (10)
St Leonard's CE Primary School, Lambeth

Seasons

In the baking hot oven that is summer,
When all the plants and leaves of trees are green,
Nature's at the peak of its beauty,
But all too soon, to fall the leaves are keen,
In summer.

When the golden leaves depart from trees in
autumn,
Sailing, soaring, swerving as the wind sighs,
As I walk across the ground, they make a
crunching, crackling sound,
And the birds sing out their wondrous song from
high,
In autumn.

As pretty flakes fall from Heaven in winter,
Those of beauty, grace, a lovely glowing white,
Cold as ice yet soft as a cake, the cold climate's
caused to make
Me wrapped up warm to stop the knife-like bite,
Of the chill in winter.

The blossoms bloom upon the trees in spring,
Those flowers full of beauty, deep, bright pink,
The start of life, pods open up to find the sun
blazing from up high,
Such allure that the world would never think of,
At any time but spring.

Patrick Hanson (10)
St Leonard's CE Primary School, Lambeth

Seasons!

Spring comes first, flowers bloom
Cars pass their fields and say *vroom!*
The golden sunflowers stand tall
Being cautious and careful not to fall.
The sun shines bright
Until it has turned to night.
Next comes summer,
It feels too hot as if it melts my brain
There is hardly any rain
I skip to the next season on a train
The season makes a path of sticks
The wooden figures let go of their golden leaves
Mischievous foxes swoop past trees
Their burning red fur flickers down to their fuzzy
tail
Fox skips into the pale
Cold, white stars fall out the sky
White, soft, cold sand lies on the ground
Melting slowly, spring is found
Flowers are reborn under the sun

Where children laugh and giggle
And there's lots of fun.

Miriam Thomas (10)

St Leonard's CE Primary School, Lambeth

The Damorth

The Damorth had: five heads and scales tough as a nail.
The Damorth had: eyes, big as trees and was a burning fiend with flaming knees.
The Damorth had: wings like a bats and a tail as long as some sails.
The Damorth had: tons of poisonous saliva and fangs like a spider's.
The Damorth had: breath of an exploding volcano and had been in many a fable.
The Damorth had: a lair full of gold and every piece was cursed.
The Damorth had: a mouth full of fifty teeth and a taste for rare beef.
The Damorth had: a hundred eyes and a head full of lies.
Would you like to be near one of its eyes?

Daniel Govier (10)
St Leonard's CE Primary School, Lambeth

Vampires

Have you heard the tale of the midnight beast?
It comes to attack at the midnight feast
There are multiple ways to kill this beast that
stalks us and eats
It loves blood but hates light and is often hunted
for bounties
No one knows if it is true, but if it is run or beat it
It is strong and the first it bites will drop their axe
and help this beast hunt at night
It is hard to spot because it can blend in and grab
you, will you grin?
Now you've heard of the tale of the midnight
beast.

Mason Davis-West (10)
St Leonard's CE Primary School, Lambeth

In My Dreams

In my dreams,
I picture different colours
Mixing and matching
Blurring and hatching
A sunrise of pink, purple and blue
And orange too
Waking up to the morning dew.

In my dreams,
Very soon...
I will see the moon
In all its power
It seems like a tower
Ever so high
I know he will never die
As he rises in the sky
I can't believe he is mine
For the night
He makes me bright
As I look at him
He shows me his shiny rim.

Emma Cox (11)
St Leonard's CE Primary School, Lambeth

Joy Of A Summer Day

The joy of a summer day,
Where the sun smiles on everyone
And the people reflect the smile.
Where the trees sway in the warm breeze,
When people are happy,
And anger and sadness are ceased
When people make water lappy
And children's shirts get creased.
When people eat a lot,
And drink as they please
When some go to the land of Scots,
And have fun with their peeps.
Young boys playing rough,
And mostly stay tough.

Timilehin Samuel Ojo (11)
St Leonard's CE Primary School, Lambeth

Anger

Anger consumes all of you
It bubbles inside you ready to blow
When you have it, you don't know what to do
It will just grow and grow.

To have it, you shouldn't be glad
Never let it take over
It will eventually make you sad
Whenever you have it, you become a loner.

Anger, it is a nightmare
It breaks your friendships in an instant
When you have it, everyone will glare
When you have it, just say a prayer.

Rocco Harrison-Hughes (10)
St Leonard's CE Primary School, Lambeth

Running

Through the trees, into the desert, into the heat
Never stopping, always running, go to the rocks
Go to the port, onto the rocks, onto the sand
Climb up the wall, to the road and there's the town
There is the sea, the beautiful sea
There is a boat, a glorious boat
Run, run, run, start up the boat into the ocean
Away, away, away,
As the sun glints and the sea shines
Lights shimmer across, I am free to run.

Ben Bourne (10)
St Leonard's CE Primary School, Lambeth

What Is The Night?

The night is a black sheet of paper
With white sparkles splashed on it
It is a very black, black sheet of mysterious paper
Every night, strange objects grow on it
The night has a huge, white, dusty ball
Ready to be the night's highlight
It's a lovely, calm, relaxing friend to have
Ever around
The night is a beautiful treasure box
How I love the night
It's magic.

Sarah Qurayshi (10)
St Leonard's CE Primary School, Lambeth

Garden

Look upon all the flowers,
See what you really desire,
Have all you can,
And treat it like an empire.
See it with one eye,
Love it with one cry,
Have it with a million bribes,
Kill it with one why,
Flowers are our lives,
Treat them like human eyes,
So before I die, I will say why.

Delissa Rhone (10)
St Leonard's CE Primary School, Lambeth

Someone Special In Life Who Has Passed Away

He loved playing with me,
In the park - eating our lunch
If I failed, I would be his lunch!
He chased me to my room,
I never wanted to go,
I wanted to stay and play some more,
Whenever I was tired, he would carry me,
His shoulders were my safe place
Dad, this will always be my memory.

Ruby Coulson (11)
St Leonard's CE Primary School, Lambeth

Brother

My brother laughs and giggles
Plays with me and my mother
He comes with me everywhere, like to Smiggle
Hugs and cries from my brother
Cheeky is my brother, but I love him anyway
Although he does annoy me
He is still my brother in the same way
So I love him and he loves me!

Nikola Motycka (10)
St Leonard's CE Primary School, Lambeth

My Wonderful Class Teacher

My wonderful class teacher
You make me smile every day
It is a joy coming to school every day
The days are sad when it's the holidays.

I am glad when you are here to help us learn
As you make us all want to learn more,
Hooray! We have got Miss Wilson!

Shiva Vishnu Govinden (10)
St Leonard's CE Primary School, Lambeth

Yellow

Yellow, my favourite colour
Yellow, my sunshine
Yellow, my hero when I am feeling sad
Yellow, my friend
Yellow, my comfort
Yellow, my cuddly toy when I am feeling mad
Yellow, the best, the thing you cannot beat
Yellow, my favourite colour.

Alysha-Kyda Musah (10)

St Leonard's CE Primary School, Lambeth

Sea

The sea is as blue as the sky
As the sun goes down and the moon goes up
The sea decorates itself with a new beat
Humans see a new light, light that shows a new
hope
The precious sea decorated with pollution with one
conclusion...

Theodore Bailey (10)
St Leonard's CE Primary School, Lambeth

Daddy

Jet-black hair he has,
My dad
Strong muscles from his workout,
At the gym.
Hazel eyes, just like mine
Folks say I look just like him,
My dad,
I'm happy with that.

Anna Laura Pereira Alberton (10)
St Leonard's CE Primary School, Lambeth

Mr Bell

There once was a man called Bell
And he was the one who felt like a shell
As soon as he fell
He began to yell
And then he did not feel well.

Dennis Epoh Moudio (10)
St Leonard's CE Primary School, Lambeth

The Mischievous Princess

I am a mischievous princess
I love to put my smelly socks
On my parents' bed and get them really angry.
Once when it was my birthday
I poured the juice on their hair
And they got mad and sent me back to my room
So I never got to have a cake again
Not even on my birthday, only presents.

Just then, one day,
It wasn't my birthday, they bought a birthday cake
And I threw it on their head
And they didn't get angry, they said it's fine
instead
They were smiling the whole time,
So I sneakily went to their room
And saw what happened to them
They had been controlled by an ugly, naughty
witch
That liked to turn people into naughty, angry
humans...

Erin Guan (8)
Trinity Primary Academy, Wood Green

Clearly

There's a world outside my door,
I don't know anymore
I'm gonna stay here now,
Close the curtains, cut the lights,
A bunch of darkness hits my mind,
It's gonna take me down,
All the roads I've been before,
Some mistakes always got me shaking,
And all the signs I once ignored,
In my denial, I didn't want to face them,
I can see clearly now,
The rain has gone
I accept all the things,
That cannot change
Gone are the dark clouds,
The dawn has come
It's gonna be a bright,
Sunshiny day,
I forced my feet down... to the ground
Take my breath,
Say my prayer,

All the pain in my sorrow
Won't change today
Only ruin tomorrow
I can see clearly now the rain has gone,
I accept all the things I cannot change,
Now it's really, just clear now.

Aleena Khan (9)
Trinity Primary Academy, Wood Green

Last Night I Dreamt Of Unicorns

Last night, I dreamt of unicorns
There were unicorns everywhere
They were galloping through the glamour hall
Annoyingly, they were eating my hair
The cheeky unicorn was against the wall, being naughty
Carelessly, they were casting a nasty spell
On my beloved cat that I loved so much.
The animals were spreading vibrant rainbows everywhere
As they raced about my comfortable bed.
The little sissy was on the couch, moving from place to place
They end up on the marvellous stairs
Happily, the unicorns were prancing around the magic carpet
Savagely, they were eating my only sock pairs
There were unicorns, unicorns, unicorns!

When I noticed I woke up today there were wonderful,
Pretty, beautiful rainbows surrounding me like I'm a celebrity.

Lamoy Olarerin (9)
Trinity Primary Academy, Wood Green

My Wonderland

I have many crazy ideas,
Some that could blow off your ears
Inviting a unicorn over for tea
Imagine how cool that would be
Doing a cool dance in your pyjamas
While talking to a bunch of disco llamas
Reading a bunch of story books
Deciding to do some art on the walls
While enjoying some tasty sausage rolls
Finished drawing the last line
Wow, I enjoyed this party of mine
I think I will go to sleep
I'll wake up before that alarm clock goes beep
That is my amazing wonderland
No, thank you, I don't need a hand.

Mariam Saada (9)
Trinity Primary Academy, Wood Green

Bizarre Wonderdream

Enchanted wind flusters my face,
I had been transported to another place!
Multicoloured sky sprinkled in sweets
Grinned like a Cheshire cat!
Huge, juicy, red mushrooms
Persuaded me to follow...

Peculiar sight surprised me
A bunch between a binny and a tiger?
Dear me, my dreams have eluded me!

Where was my fate leading?
To trees, to bees, to keys...

I open the entrance and wave goodbye
The day was beginning while my eyes were
opening.

Goodbye, my bizarre dream!

Marsilda Peposhi (10)
Trinity Primary Academy, Wood Green

Dream Land

Where all the knights and dragons lay
A different world above the clouds and space
Where not even stars can reach
Where you can roam free
Where time's upside down
And tea is at three
Where there's no school and no visas
Lollipop rivers flowing through
Where dreams come true and flow through the air
Laughter and giggles surrounding you
There's no homework too
Where you can take bubble baths
In the chocolate river
This is my dream
And you can join me too.

Luna Tomas (9)
Trinity Primary Academy, Wood Green

My Cat Tom

My cat's name is Tom,
He's furry like a pom-pom,
He likes to chew a bat,
Just like a normal cat.

He's always furry
And will never hurry,
Tom plays with toys
Like normal boys.

My cat is a brother to me,
As you can simply see,
He plays a lot,
Just as a fun robot.

Tom won't leave my side,
He would never hide,
Tom is my cat
And he sleeps on my mat.

Vanousheh Abdi (9)
Trinity Primary Academy, Wood Green

What A Wonderful Day!

What a wonderful day!
What should I do today?
I know, I'll go out and play!
I say hi to he and hi to she
But then I see...

What?
Whatever can it be?
Do I believe what I see?
It's a talking tree!
And...

What?
Whatever is that?
It's an... invisible cat!

Well, I guess it's not so grand
But what do you expect
We are in Wonderland!

Katrina Poveda (10)
Trinity Primary Academy, Wood Green

Strange Little Feather

There is a little feather
Her name is Heather
She has dimples
But also some pimples
She always smiles
When she has liked a teacher's files
This was the story of Heather
A naughty little feather.

Leah Mpofu (9)
Trinity Primary Academy, Wood Green

Alien Invasion

She has arrows coming out of her head
Interacting with aliens
One day, she will rise up
Like a spider and will take over the world
Will we survive the invasion?

Faysal Ghebbache (10)
Trinity Primary Academy, Wood Green

Playing On Magina

I'm walking
I'm looking
At hot lava
I'm sliding
On the rings
I'm jumping
On bumpy rocks
So happy!

Muhammad Ibrahim Kayani (6)

Trinity Primary Academy, Wood Green

Ocean

O pen the tree in the sea door
C lownfish jump to the sun
E very time I dream in the sea
A nything can swim in the seaweed
N ever get a mermaid in a net because they drown.

Kemi Ogunnubi-Sime (6)
Vauxhall Primary School, Vauxhall

Ocean

O pen the magic and creepy castle
C lownfish creep around and look for food
E normous sparkling sea
A crobatic jellyfish jiggle
N ight-time sharks go out and hunt for food.

Sibella Harvey (6)
Vauxhall Primary School, Vauxhall

Ocean

O pen the enchanted kingdom
C razy whale sharks creeping in the ocean
E nchanted treasure chest opened
A wesome amazing animals
N aughty whales swimming through the sea.

Lucas Ngo (6)
Vauxhall Primary School, Vauxhall

Ocean

O pen the secret pearl
C ourtney is a mermaid you see!
E normous watermelon pack
A mazing spectacular diamond
N ight, the little kingdom shines bright, wow wee!

Courtney Bezzina (6)
Vauxhall Primary School, Vauxhall

Ocean

O pen the scary treasure chest
C lownfish are really funny
E xcited fish are funny
A dventures in the sea are scary
N et fishes in the sea are scary.

Dana Meho (6)
Vauxhall Primary School, Vauxhall

Ocean

O ne octopus dances in the shower
C reepy fishes are scary
E very rude shark
A aliyah is a shark
N ear November, we have a party in the ocean.

Aaliyah Taylor (6)
Vauxhall Primary School, Vauxhall

Ocean

O pen the shark's mouth
C rawling slow snails seek
E normous whales bathing in the sea
A mazing colourful starfish
N ight-time is creepy.

Blessing Oluwatofunmi Akinola (6)
Vauxhall Primary School, Vauxhall

Ocean

O ctopus with dotted spots
C rabs with orange claws but no paws
E nchanted kingdom ahead
A n African mermaid named Marie
N ever swim alone!

Marie Moore (6)
Vauxhall Primary School, Vauxhall

Ocean

O pen the magical fun chest
C an bubbles live?
E normous shark eats the sand
A merican mermaid called Emily
N ever-ending, cool adventure.

Yasmin Seisay (7)
Vauxhall Primary School, Vauxhall

Ocean

O pen the fish's mouth
C reepy picture moving in the sea
E ating the salty sea
A crazy octopus moving
N o one is in the sea.

Guney Yilmaz (6)
Vauxhall Primary School, Vauxhall

Ocean

O pen the secret cage
C razy cupcakes are in the sea
E at a shark in the sea
A person is making a BBQ!
N ight is very strange.

Joanelle Oppong-Boateng (6)
Vauxhall Primary School, Vauxhall

Ocean

O pen the enchanted chest
C razy crabs creep
E nchanted crazy sharks
A wesome crazy stingray
N oisy crazy whales.

Jonah Ennis (6)
Vauxhall Primary School, Vauxhall

Ocean

O ne magical shark
C an you see the scary
E erie fairy?
A re you a sea urchin
N ew mermaid or creepy clown shark?

Eesah Kyriacou (6)
Vauxhall Primary School, Vauxhall

Ocean

O ne pirate is sick
C reepy treasure chest
E nter the creepy door
A pirate was being chased
N obody helped him.

Miyah Morris Doyle (6)
Vauxhall Primary School, Vauxhall

Norwegian Man

There was once a smelly, lazy man
Who was shorter than a frying pan
He came from Norway in the north
He wanted to go further forth
He picked a mushroom from the ground
And said, "I wonder what I've found."
He put the mushroom in his mouth
It picked him up and flung him south
As you know, the south is cold
And this lazy man was very old
Then the fungi quickly grew
But instead of red, it turned out blue!
The stout man was about to be
Involved in a catastrophe
Then he popped like a balloon
Whizzing him to cold Neptune
Where he met an alien
Calling himself, Smailion
This is where he will end
But his next adventure is round the bend.

George Blick (10)
Wendell Park Primary School, White City

A Crack In The Sky

There's a crack in the sky!
There's a crack in the sky!
It glowed as it hit the night
Giving everyone a tremendous fright
Its smooth, yet cracked edges
Made most people run to the hedges
Its loud, malicious moan
Made the brave ones simply groan
Suddenly, it got bigger!
As the world got thinner
It was being sucked into that crack
It was a magnet forcing life to get sucked in!
And not missing the smallest thing
As I got sucked in
The world turned upside down
The trees were blue and the sky was green
My life was oh so serene
Then I woke up!
In an old hospital bed
Was it all a dream?
Well that, I don't know.

Noah Foxwell (9)
Wendell Park Primary School, White City

There Was A Man

There was a man sitting on a sun
He made a letter, the letter made fun
There was a big sun
A man came back
He was writing a letter
But one day, something was bad
So that's when he...

Jaylen Durojaiye (9)
Wendell Park Primary School, White City

Computer Problem!

"I love Fortnite!" shouted Jack,
Who used to play on a Mac
Jack was thirteen and very, very kind
If someone asked for something,
He wouldn't even mind!
One day, Jack's computer started shaking,
He thought it was breaking!
Suddenly, Jack was sucked into his computer,
He stood confused, very much
He saw the Fortnite icon and it opened with a touch!
Next, he played a game of Fortnite and fell from the sky
He threw his glider and threw his red tie!
He picked up a sniper rifle and it was yellow,
Jack shot a player and was instantly eliminated,
The player bellowed, "How could this happen to me?"
Jack jumped out of his huge, fast computer,
He drank some water,
Then he sat on his chair.

Mohammod Dua Mahmud Unnoto (10)
Whittingham Primary Academy, Walthamstow

The Gummy Bear's Adventure

G ross dribble was coming out of my mouth, suddenly I woke up

U nbelievably, I drank from my cup

M y body turned to a gummy bear and I was in a rocket

M oaning, "Why do I have to be a gummy bear?" when I saw a bucket

Y *uck*, I threw it out of the window

B ut I decided to put on a layer of clothes

E xhausted, I went to the window - it turned into a doughnut!

A nd it was flying towards me - suddenly, I decided to eat a nut

R unning around the rocket to see if anyone was there

S uddenly, I decided I should sit on a chair

A nd no one came, I took the matter into my hands

D uring me getting ready, it became clear I needed to be careful

V iciously, I climbed out of the spaceship

E ventually, I got there, I acted like we had a type of friendship

N ow it slowed down

T ill finally, I started to eat it and it all went to belly town

U nbelievably, I just saved myself by eating!

R acing back to the space rocket, I felt amazing

E ventually, I went to bed, woke up, and realised it was all a dream - wow!

Chloe Alexandra Bray (9)
Whittingham Primary Academy, Walthamstow

Sun, Lawyers And Geese

Arghhhh, it's so cold!
Even more than the North Pole
The light has fallen into darkness
And the sun has become unstarted.

A crazy dude
With a big clue
Decides to build a machine
To freeze the solar system
An on and off button has been made
To continue the past of the Ice Age.

Lawyers, lawyers, lawyers,
Hunting, hunting, hunting,
Searching all the fun things
Except bee stings.
"They won't find me."
"It would be easier to find a green pea."

Frozen and fearful,
A golden goose,
Starving and searching
Has finally been perching

Inside an old garage
On top of a parcel.

Inside the parcel
In the garage
Are two mega buttons
Much bigger than mutton
Lawyers are nearby
Hearing lots of lies.

"Quack!" hurls the geese,
The lawyers have a peek
And find the machine
On top is a goose,
Resting in peace.

Arghhhh, it's so hot!
Even more in a pot
The light has arrived to brightness
And the sun has started once more.

Mary Luggie (10)
Whittingham Primary Academy, Walthamstow

Marshmallow Dinosaurs On The Loose!

People say dinosaurs were big,
And didn't live with humans!
Well, actually, that's not true!
In fact, they weren't just dinosaurs,
They were marshmallow dinosaurs...
They had a very big head,
With a big, fat marshmallow body.

People say dinosaurs were scary
And very scaly and chased other dinosaurs,
Well, that's not true, in fact
They were very fluffy and friendly
And they lived with humans!

People say dinosaurs would eat humans
If they were still alive
And step on everyone,
Well, that's not true
They had soft feet

And were even human's pets
And I even had one myself!

People say dinosaurs were big
And didn't live with humans!
Well, actually, that's not true,
But the reason they're not here is because
An asteroid hit the planet and all
The marshmallow dinosaurs melted into little bits!

Anabel Amaka Chinedu (10)

Whittingham Primary Academy, Walthamstow

Oh Buttons, Buttons Why?

A boring day on the step
I went down to the kitchen to feed my pet
Then I saw this door and a button key
Thought, *well maybe I should go in there*, so I did
I got the key, opened the door and went in
In there was a strange door again
Then I found myself in...
Button Land!
How strange!
When I arrived, everything was so small
That I could even touch the clouds
When I was going to touch the cloud
There was a cookie
So I just ate it!
Suddenly, I shrank
Into a tiny ant!
Oh no!
I'd shrunk, oh well!
Then everything was buttons
"Oh my! That's so cool!"
But, just then, I noticed I became all buttons

Then I flew off to the moon somehow
And lived there forever!

Emma Dervishi (9)
Whittingham Primary Academy, Walthamstow

My Favourite Wish

I was wishing for a dragon,
that could fly really high,
and then, *poof!*
There was a dragon in the sky!
He put me on his back,
but in space there was a gigantic rock,
a meteor hit us and we fell!
I then wished that we were safe,
then the dragon flew through a portal out of
space.

We went inside
It was really a fantastic ride!
Then, somehow, my annoying sister came with me,
then I wished that I was free,
but then I saw a shining crown,
but closer and closer,
I knew that it was the Queen of cards!
But then I fell through a rabbit hole,
and then I didn't know where to go!
I then fell on my bed, I knew it was a dream!
and then I rested my tired, sleepy head

Luis James Calde (9)
Whittingham Primary Academy, Walthamstow

United Unicorn!

United Unicorn flying through the street,
Looking for a tasty treat,
Walking in the sky,
We flew to Upside Down Land,
Which was made out of sand,
It was born in June, which would come very soon,
But then a monster appeared,
We ran away, but it followed us,
It gnashed its teeth,
We were probably its midnight feast,
But suddenly, it became day and it flew away,
It came again, but now with its daughter,
I jumped off for a slaughter,
My United Unicorn came to me,
And swept me off my feet,
It took me to Chocolate World,
It landed on a strong, thick cloud,
But the monster came again that night,
And we flew to the land of light,
Which banished him with all of his fright.

Alexander Chan Krinickas (8)
Whittingham Primary Academy, Walthamstow

Hive Jungle Adventure

As I crept out the rabbit hole,
I fell through a passage of mossy stone.
There, I saw a big black mole as big as a dragon,
Deep down was a jungle with hanging vines,
Lots of new animals like flyzards.

Moley, the mole,
That I met in the hole,
At Dripping Drop Lake,
Hot like it was baked,
The mossy rocks made it look like a mountain.

Split, split, split, the hive was breaking,
Honey blobs were floating around,
Bananas flew away as fast as possible.
Bang! Bang! Crash! It was a crazy, chaotic disaster,
Vines fell from the sky.

The life magic was gone,
Gone, gone, gone,
The bananas repaired everything,
I smelled to check.

David Tinculescu (8)
Whittingham Primary Academy, Walthamstow

In The Chamber Of Secrets For 72 Hours

C hamber of Secrets I'm going to live in
H ow, oh how did I get in here?
A lso, what am I going to eat?
M aybe just some dirty water
B ut in the chamber, there is a *big* secret
E arlier, when I came in
R oaring noises were heard

O ut of nowhere comes a huge monster
F rightened, I am

S adly, I can't see my friends
E ven they can't come in to say hi
C racking noises are heard
R eally scared, I am
E ven when there are dripping noises
T alking, I am, a lot!
S uddenly, I wake up, it was all a dream...

Daniel Brace Carmona (9)
Whittingham Primary Academy, Walthamstow

Crazy Land

At the end of the day,
my cousin ran away.
I saw a rabbit,
he had a good habit.
He was very mad,
but he loved his toy.
He went down the hole,
but he still jumped with his toy.

He jumped down, which was too long,
but his ears were folded.
When I saw the world,
I found a huge mole.
I said, "Argh! This world is great!"
I ate my marshmallow,
with a bellow.

I climbed up a tree,
but I fell down with a sneeze,
then I tried to make a candy ladder,
but I broke it with a hammer.

I was very angry,
so my tummy was rumbling,
I made a cake,
and it exploded in my face,
I said I would stay here forever!

Antonio Georoiav (9)

Whittingham Primary Academy, Walthamstow

Candy Land!

One beautiful day
I went on my way...
Until I fell down a rabbit hole
I looked at where I was
It was full of sweets
I couldn't wait
What would I meet?
I could not believe what I was seeing
It was not even a human being
She was a unicorn
Then, within a few minutes, we ate popcorn
After, we ate bubble flow
We just had to blow
There were sweets inside the bubbles
I really wanted to cuddle
The bubble popped
The lollipop went down
I really wanted to drown
The unicorn said she was going to a trampoline
I thought, *where is the trampoline?*

I saw her jumping on some jelly
It made a grumble in my belly.

Stacey Li (8)
Whittingham Primary Academy, Walthamstow

Vomiting Cupcakes

I went for a walk
I started to talk
A crooked magic stick fell into my mouth
I don't know why but I started to shout!
I went to bed and when I woke up I felt sick
Then I remembered I had eaten the stick!
After, something magical happened...
I started to vomit cupcakes!

V omiting
O oooh!
M essy
I vomited cupcakes
T asted delicious
I vomited cupcakes
N ooo!
G ooey

C upcakes
U nbelievable
P erfectly decorated

C upcakes
A mazing
K elly now thinks I am weird
E llie does not like it
S ticky!

Bodhi-Rae Breathnatch (7)
Whittingham Primary Academy, Walthamstow

My True Love Brought Me...

One day,
on Monday,
my true love said,
"I brought you some flowers."

One day,
on Tuesday,
my true love brought me,
a cat.

One day,
on Wednesday,
my true love brought me,
a big white polar bear.

One day,
on Thursday,
my true love brought me,
a pink apple lollipop.

One day,
on Friday,
my true love brought me,
a pink iPad and phone...

And I said,
"Do I need this much stuff in my house?"

And my true love said...
"I brought you some chocolate!"

"What did I just say?
Argh!"

Kacper Kajetan Baginski (8)
Whittingham Primary Academy, Walthamstow

Meeting Santa!

I woke up in the living room and heard a sound,
I thought it might be my mum trying on a gown,
Then I saw Santa pop right up in front of my eyes,
Instead of getting my present from Santa, I thought of pies,
I thought of getting a plushie, but I didn't even bother,
If Santa was here then the noise was Rudolph, could he hover?

Then I asked, "Why are you here?"
After, I teleported onto a pier!
Then, after a while, I saw a dolphin swimming across the pier,
When I looked up, I saw a deer floating across the sky,
I shouted, "OMG, a deer!"

Now how could this day get any worse?

Scarlett Chan (7)
Whittingham Primary Academy, Walthamstow

Crazy Wonderland

As I crept out of the rabbit hole,
I felt something enjoyable and fun.
Everything was bubbling with burgers,
Filling me with ideas to jump on them.
As big as a palace!
As tall as a crane!
And then I found an adorable alien,
A purple one insane,
With slimy colours.
It was called Hamza,
A three-eyed monster,
Then I jumped on the burgers, *boing, boing, boing,*
And ended up in space...
I saw a burger Saturn!
Boing, boing, boing...
What was that?
I saw Saturn's rings, flat!
No, too bubbly!
And from then on, I called the planet 'Burger'.

Miran Beter (9)
Whittingham Primary Academy, Walthamstow

River Wye And River Usk

R iver was brownish like Usk when,
I t got browner and browner,
V alley a few miles away,
E very day it was brownish,
R iver Wye flew part Usk.

W ye looks after River Wye,
Y ou will never run away,
E very day, River Wye is the best.

R iver Usk has sand on the sides when,
I t flies past River Wye,
V iewing Usk from a hill,
E very time it happens,
R iver Usk is the best.

U sk is close to River Wye,
S un makes it brown all the time,
K arate fun with the waves.

Joris Kasperavicius (7)
Whittingham Primary Academy, Walthamstow

Talking Island

As I fell down the rabbit hole,
I saw something white and plain,
Heard a loud growl like a thunder strike,
Also felt a tickle beneath my feet,
When I came out of the rabbit hole, I landed on,
A big island, freaky and freezing,
Brr, it got colder and colder,
Then a lip came and kept on saying 'Galbert'.
Suddenly, a whole army of little lips kept on saying 'Galbert'!
They started getting on me and then I became a lip,
Also saying 'Galbert' all the time.
When I woke up, I just realised it was a dream,
But then I kept on saying, 'Grasbobly'!

Gabby Bonsu (8)

Whittingham Primary Academy, Walthamstow

Sweetie Wonderland

Sugar canes and Skittles rain,
Lollipops and fizzy pops
Yummy Nerdz and chocolate birds
Welcome to Sweetie Wonderland!

Fruity Fruitella and bread with Nutella,
Sour floors and candy doors,
Sticky fingers and mouth tinglers,
Come and live in Sweetie Wonderland!

Toxic waste makes your heart race
Juicy drop pop makes your stomach pop
Jelly beans and choco-tangerines
Welcome to Sweetie Wonderland!

Candy sticks and chocolate chips
Chocolate Thorntons and raspberry bonbons
Sour feet and gummy sweets
Come and live in Sweetie Wonderland!

Mariama Abdiwahab (10)
Whittingham Primary Academy, Walthamstow

Life Of A Sad Future

Tables and pencils telling me
I will have a bad future
I don't know what to say
I am just having a bad day
Telling me my life will be
In a world with no happiness
That's for me full of sadness
A place with no homes
It's not good, I need someone
To support me
Oh, just give me a cup of tea
It will be full of creatures
And maybe, a poisonous snake
That knows how to bake.

It is scary, no fairies, just giants
That are dear, no school
I am just gonna be a fool
That's not cool and
The worst thing, no pools!

Adam Aziz (10)
Whittingham Primary Academy, Walthamstow

The Octopus Girl

There was once a man and a squid
They fell in love and had a daughter called Sid
She was born in December
Even the fish remembered
Also, Ursula was her aunt
And she never took it for granted
One time, she went exploring
Because the rain was pouring
And she saw a blue fish
Which was her favourite dish
She took it to her mum
And she said, "Oh, you little plum,
That's a piece of rubbish
I'm making blueblack fish
Isn't that your favourite dish?"
"Yes, it is
And I love it when it goes *fizz!*"

Alev Ekrem (9)
Whittingham Primary Academy, Walthamstow

A Wonderful World Of Fantasy

Crazy unicorns dashing through the woods
A lucky person waited for the keys
Then a cat came there and stood
The children came rushing to see

Under the ocean, there was a rumble and a thump
Next, I saw my friend looking shocked
I fell and I think my head had a bump
Candy keys fell out of the sky and some popped!

Oh no! Here it comes
We were all surprised
A boy said he was number one
The unicorn didn't mind

Screaming rainbows attacked
The unicorns ran
Not to mention the fact
That children played in the sun.

Mahira Shara (9)
Whittingham Primary Academy, Walthamstow

The Monkey Tail Land

M onkey tails point up high
O n the monkey tails, spiders crawl up high
N atural plants grow tall and strong
K eys fly until they break
E lephant's trunks spray water
Y ellow bananas getting eaten by monkeys

T ails fly everywhere
A nimals jump side to side
I nsects that fly land on trees
L ands full of monkeys

L adybirds fly everywhere
A nimals land on trees
N atural plants grow up high
D ragonflies fly everywhere.

Shayma Mohammed (9)
Whittingham Primary Academy, Walthamstow

Space

In the hot morning
A little monster went to Mars
He blasted off with fresh milk
It was colder than snow
Blasting off into the Milky Way.

He saw stars playing
Before the chocolate sun got them.
There came one
It took three stars, the strongest
Sent to blast his laser gun and zap him
Into a million blue pieces.

He finally reached the Chocy Wars
He thought it was made out of chocolate chips
Volcanoes erupted with hot chocolate.
The moon was made of cheese
With milk inside the holes.

Leovardo Daniel Jayden Thompson (7)
Whittingham Primary Academy, Walthamstow

Harry The Homework Eater

Step by step
Out he's crept
Just to lurk
Out for homework
His name is Harry
There is no worry
He is unique
Out he goes to seek
He makes no noise
Be careful, he loves toys

Step by step
Out he's crept
Sometimes under your sofa
Well, it might be Harry the homework eater
You might be happy
But if not, you might be lucky
He has a big appetite
So beware of what you see in your sight

He is never sick or old
Even if he feels poor and cold.

Anis Chebbab (9)
Whittingham Primary Academy, Walthamstow

Candy Land!

One step here
One step there
Marshmallow people everywhere
Tangerine rivers and pink lemonade pools
This serves me right
I'm going on vacation!
Peppermint hills
You don't even need to pay bills!
Forget about vacation
'Cause I'm living here!
Don't think about stopping me
As I will burst into gummies!
Imagination is wild
But this is next level!
I think it's just a dream
But I can never be sure
You should even see the rock clear candy floor!

Taybah Zainab Shah (9)
Whittingham Primary Academy, Walthamstow

The Evil Unicorn Catches The Girl!

Her fur was the darkest of red,
but she never went to bed.
At midnight, she was very awake,
but in the day, she was okay.
The evil unicorn, Dark Sparkle, met a girl,
then the unicorn's fur shone like a scaly fleece.
She leapt towards the girl with rage,
then she turned dark beige!
Then the girl ran away,
and never went back again.
Then she appeared in another land called
Inversland,
and stayed there for her whole life.
For dinner, she had rice,
after her day of fright.

Sirena Hinds (8)
Whittingham Primary Academy, Walthamstow

Shops In...

As I crept out of the rabbit hole,
I felt something slimy and cold,
I was in a place which was white,
Something was in sight,
It smelt like smoke,
I felt a poke,
It was a dishonest, dangerous dragon!
I ran for my life,
But it ate me in one go,
Crunch!
I went down into his tummy,
"Woah!"
When I landed,
Something caught my eye,
There were many shops,
Underneath his beef chops,
Well, no wonder he was so fat!

Martha Elsie Sennett (8)
Whittingham Primary Academy, Walthamstow

Evil Humans

Evil, evil Pokémon!
Pikachu saves Ash and electrocutes the evil
Pokémon
Thunder comes out of his cheeks
Good Pokémon are friends with Ash
Pikachu screams!
He kills the other good Pokémon
Ash gets Pikachu another Pokémon to help him
Legend Charizard is chosen
"Charizard, I choose you!"
Ash told Legend Charizard to use fireball
Pikachu and Legend Charizard won!

Kayden Cooke (7)
Whittingham Primary Academy, Walthamstow

Candy Land!

I was in Candy Land, but,
It was full of burgers!
I saw a scare,
Hairs everywhere!
It flew away,
But it would come back another day.
While I was there, I ate the burger,
But I was still in hunger...

I missed my dad,
So I went back,
Just because of that,
My parents missed me too,
So should you!

I flew back to my parents in May,
Hopefully I would come back another day!

Mia Bondzie (8)
Whittingham Primary Academy, Walthamstow

The Crazy Water-Breathing Dragon

As I crept out of the rabbit hole,
I felt something wet and cold,
Could it be?
The sea!
I couldn't really see,
Anything, except an underwater barbecue,
And... and a dragon?
Suddenly, I saw two lights coming to me,
It was a submarine!
It said, "Pay £1000 for swimming!"
So I dashed away,
After, I found myself in a bucket that said 'Prey'!

Youcef Kaizra (8)
Whittingham Primary Academy, Walthamstow

A Magical Kingdom

I was in a magical land,
It was like a dream.
There were golden unicorns,
Candies were dancing,
The land had rainbows that were singing,
It was so much fun,
A unicorn had a flower bun.

There was a flying cookie,
There was a unicorn called Bookie,
Me and Bookie were hanging out,
I began to shout,
There weren't any vets,
Once unicorn was wet.

Nisa Altun (8)
Whittingham Primary Academy, Walthamstow

Meeting Santa

I was about to sleep
But I heard a *bang, bang, bang*
So I went downstairs
I opened the door and I saw Santa
I was so happy when I saw him!

I was playing in the snow
And I saw a dragon
And it was a fire dragon
I wanted to ride the dragon.

Then I saw people having a barbecue
So I joined in the fun
After, Santa took me home.

Ariana Alexandra Vacaru (7)
Whittingham Primary Academy, Walthamstow

The Wobbly Jelly

In a land of wobbly jelly
Little creatures live
You will see
Little creatures pop out of the land
The little wobbly jelly creatures slide down
I can't believe it!
I see the creatures laughing and laughing again
I start to laugh as well!
I never saw anything slide down a wobbly jelly
before.
I go back home
And wish I can go there again.

Chelsea Li (7)
Whittingham Primary Academy, Walthamstow

The Terrifying Pencil

I met a little pencil,
who gave me a stare,
had a lair,
did not care,
looked like a bear,
gave me a scare,
sat on a chair,
did a dare.
He had teeth,
loved beef,
hated leaves,
he wanted to be a chief.
He had eyes,
told lies.
He had a nose,
he chose,
he had hairs,
hated chairs,
loved bears.

Elle May Newman (8)
Whittingham Primary Academy, Walthamstow

Apple Flossing

One time, I saw an apple tree
Then I saw an apple coming out
I saw the apple growing legs and arms
He was about to do something
He was doing the floss
He couldn't stop flossing
And I couldn't eat him
I brought him home
And he was still flossing.

Jameer Cadotco (7)
Whittingham Primary Academy, Walthamstow

Dancing Shoes

This dancing shoe is driving me crazy
But he dances tip-top amazing
On the dusty shelf
It's really his self
He says, "Tip-top, tip-top," all day long
He tiptoes a ballet all day long
But one day, we saw a shoe disaster
I ran faster.

Elitza Georgieva (8)

Whittingham Primary Academy, Walthamstow

Rain Chicks

So fun in the sun
But today it is raining chicks
Cute and cuddly
Cuddly and snuggly, catch them all!

Lovely, snuggly and fluffy
I love this town, I will never frown
Rain or brains, always the same.

Tamara Kuneva (7)
Whittingham Primary Academy, Walthamstow

![YoungWriters Est. 1991]

Young Writers Information

We hope you have enjoyed reading this book – and that you will continue to in the coming years.

If you're a young writer who enjoys reading and creative writing, or the parent of an enthusiastic poet or story writer, do visit our website **www.youngwriters.co.uk**. Here you will find free competitions, workshops and games, as well as recommended reads, a poetry glossary and our blog. There's lots to keep budding writers motivated to write!

If you would like to order further copies of this book, or any of our other titles, then please give us a call or visit **www.youngwriters.co.uk**.

Young Writers
Remus House
Coltsfoot Drive
Peterborough
PE2 9BF
(01733) 890066
info@youngwriters.co.uk

Join in the conversation!
Tips, news, giveaways and much more!

 YoungWritersUK    @YoungWritersCW